UNMASKED

UNMASKED

AUTOBIOGRAPHY
of GERRY CHEEVERS

as told to MARC ZAPPULLA

SPORTS IMPROPER PUBLICATIONS

Unmasked
Gerry Cheevers and Marc Zappulla
Sports Improper Publications
Copyright © 2011 Sports Improper Publications
Cataloging information

ISBN-13: 978-0-9843845-3-2
ISBN-10: 0-9843845-3-7

Printed in the United States

Contents

Gerry Cheevers

Foreword

Every team needs a player like Gerry Cheevers and every player needs a teammate like Gerry Cheevers. In my years of observing teams as teams, or players as players, no one has so unwittingly been able to affect the mood or mindset like Cheevers. Somehow, Gerry was able to bring a calmness, intensity, loyalty, trust, accountability, attitude and, oh yes, humor without openly trying to accomplish it. His ability to perform at the highest level, of course, was necessary for all his mysterious influences to be effective, both as a player and coach.

Unmasked is more than just a story of Gerry's travels and travails on his way to the top. It is a candid and frank account of the realities of life for a boy determined to make it to the NHL. His journey, as described, could be applied to countless young hopefuls with the same aspirations. Some were successful; most were not.

Gerry tells you his personal tale, but reveals what was necessary during the decades from 1950 through 1980 for most young men with their minds and eyes set on the NHL. This delightful chronicle allows the reader to understand how a career was forged during these years. The path to hockey success is a different one today, and will never again be as the one Gerry Cheevers had to follow.

Unmasked brings smiles to our faces and laughter to our hearts. It is pure joy for the reader.

Gerry Cheevers is the perfect one to let us in on his wonderful experience.

~ Harry Sinden

A Letter from Cheesie

There's no ego trip here, or personal vendettas brought forward and displayed in this book for everyone to see. What you're about to read is simply a story about a goaltender and his career. Though my experiences may share a likeness with the many others who played in the era I did, what makes it unique is that this is my story.

~ Gerry Cheevers

Introduction

Unmasked is the story of Gerry Cheevers, a man's journey which began within the amiable boundaries of St. Catharines, Ontario, Canada, and culminated with the hoisting of hockey's most storied treasure, Lord Stanley's Cup.

He was talented, so talented. His firm insistence to never give in to defeat would propel him to a greatness celebrated by hockey fans from all over the world.

This man would be known as a "money goaltender," the quintessential big-game player. For twenty-one years, justifiably so, Gerald Michael "Cheesie" Cheevers held close the burden of being then one of the top goaltenders his sport has ever seen.

For more than two decades Cheevers competed with unyielding grit, a rugged, hard-nosed style that will forever be deep rooted in the hearts of hockey fans everywhere. But off the ice he is marked by benevolence, a kindhearted nature with an often exhibited touch of hilarity. He is a "character," as described by many of his friends over the years. But more importantly, he is a proud husband to his wife, Betty; a loving father to his kids, Craig, Sherril, and Robby; and a beloved grandfather to his grandchildren, Laura, Cate, Jonathon, and Julianna.

His journey began on the ponds of St. Catharines, Ontario, an urban metropolis located in Canada's Niagara Region. He played his first professional game with the Toronto Maple Leafs, and when it became clear that the organization was already loaded with quality goaltending, Cheevers became the odd man out. Subsequently, he signed with the Boston Bruins, where he transcended as a goaltender and became a two-time Stanley Cup champion. Following his retirement as a player in 1980 due to a knee injury, Cheevers found himself calling the shots behind the Bruins' bench as their head coach for four and a half years, finishing with an impressive .604 winning percentage. In 1985, accordingly, Gerry Cheevers would be inducted into the Hockey Hall of Fame.

The man considered one of hockey's all-time greats recounts his entire life in majestic detail, with an upright adoration for the game he loved. He offers genuine candor about all the people he encountered while a professional hockey player, on and off the ice, in this, his first ever autobiography.

Although in this brief synopsis you'll gather a career filled with marvel, conquests, and recognition, Gerry Cheevers will be the first one to tell us all that his journey to the top was nothing short of an arduous one. His hometown Toronto Maple Leafs did not need him. He spent years in the minors with the Bruins, blurring his fate to a degree in which the well traveled net minder nearly called it quits. But after logging in almost 400 games on hockey's most humble terrain, Boston would name him their starting goaltender.

Out of his days in black and gold came a mask which would be identified with grit and character, and would carry a prolonged existence in the hearts of hockey fans everywhere. The mysteries surrounding the mask, including its origins and most startling facts, as well as where it rests this very day, will be unveiled in this book.

Unmasked is a story of one man's climb to hockey's summit. It is about the obstacles he encountered, and how he overcame them to become a champion. This book was written in honor of the game he loves, his fans, his friends, and most of all, his family, for their everlasting support through the years.

Gerry Cheevers' daring style behind the net has remained a remembrance of purity in the game of hockey; his mask, a symbol of lore; and his triumphs, firmly embedded in hockey's most treasured history. With this book, this man's story now comes to life.

Marc Zappulla
May 2011

ST. CATHARINES

I was just a kid, maybe eight years of age; young and tough, and eager to play hockey. I was eager to win.

I was a member of the St. Denis Shamrocks Church team, an expansion club in the Catholic Youth Organization (CYO) in St. Catharines and my dad was the coach. I played forward the first game and failed to register a point. Sadly, my teammates, each one of them, shared my regrettable fate as we were taken apart that day 18–0. When the following contest was upon us, my dad, the crafty guru of all that's hockey, put me between the pipes.

I can't recall my father having any intuitive sense of my ability as a future goaltender. His decision did come easy, though. His rationale: He had no desire to put anyone in net aside from his son, and the poor goalie who let eighteen slip past him in the previous game never showed up. That fact meant little in the interim as we were thrashed in game two, 15–0.

I had no time to weep or wonder as dad penciled me back in goal.

Discouragement, though, that is something I never embraced. I played with no mask, no fear then, only the desire to win. I met each attacker head on with the same intensity in my first game as a kid, as I did in my last game as a professional.

I relished my time in net as a young boy; clearly, I never left.

I was born and raised in the urban area of St. Catharines, Ontario, in the heart of the Niagara Falls region, about sixty or so miles from Toronto, just across Lake Ontario.

My folks were both Canadian born. My dad, Joe Cheevers, was a great athlete and hall of fame lacrosse player in the Heartland Province. And though he never got paid much in the sport, lacrosse was a relevant part of his life, as it was for a lot of folks across the vast northern tundra of Canada.

As the breadwinner in the family, dad was one of the top car salesmen in all of Canada, as well as the Assistant Manager of the St. Catharines Arena. And he would later become a scout for the Toronto Maple Leafs.

Bette Cheevers, my mom, would stay home and raise us kids. There were three of us: Me; my brother, Pat; and my sister, God rest her soul, Sally. She passed away too soon at the age of two after succumbing to Cystic Fibrosis.

My mother wasn't a big hockey fan, but she knew what was going on. She went to all my games when I was a kid, but ended that trend when I relocated from St. Catharines to Toronto to play at the junior level.

My aunt and grandparents on my dad's side were the only other relatives I had in St. Catharines.

Despite its quasi remoteness, life for me, as a kid in Ontario, would be anything but anomalous.

As early as I can remember I was wearing skates and playing hockey. Every other house in the neighborhood had some sort of patchwork icy expanse we could call a rink, so finding a pick-up game was trouble-free to say the least. My dad would build one across the street from where I grew up; accessibility was perpetual. Quite frankly, if someone took a stroll down my street back then, they'd probably find a makeshift rink every third or fourth house down. And playing hockey as much as we did wasn't isolated to the area where I grew up—that was the culture in Ontario and the rest of Canada.

So if we weren't tearing up someone's backyard, practicing at the rink, or playing street hockey, we'd be skating at the nearest pond. It's what we did after school until our parents rang the dinner bell.

Through our devotion to hockey, naturally, a lot of us would pay mind to the ones who lit the lamps in the NHL. The only problem of course was that we couldn't see them; we could only hear them over the radio. The airwaves were busy each night in most households across Canada.

Then, we had a breakthrough.

The NHL began broadcasting one regular season game every Saturday night. It began in the early 1950s and they called the show Hockey Night in Canada. Hockey was just making the jump from radio to television. Families from all over Canada would stay home on Saturday nights and huddle around the television set to watch just a period and a half of the NHL's finest. That's all we got, no more, due to the television restrictions.

It was an exciting time. I can still hear Foster Hewitt, the famed broadcaster of Hockey Night in Canada, begin his telecast by saying, "Hello, Canada, and hockey fans in the United States and Newfoundland…"

You couldn't match the excitement in any other country that considers their national sport their main export; it just won't happen.

For me, it was an aesthetic delight, and an opportunity to enjoy some of my favorite NHL players in action.

Although, personally, I didn't have many heroes on the ice to emulate, but if I had to choose one, it would have been Walter "Turk" Broda.

Broda was a longtime net minder for the Toronto Maple Leafs and one of the great goaltenders the NHL had ever seen. He was a man to look up to for the youngsters in St Catharines and the rest of Ontario. It was every kid's dream from my area to eventually play hockey for the Leafs and Broda was one of their biggest stars. He spent all of his years as a professional goaltender with the Leafs, winning the Vezina Trophy twice, and taking home Lord Stanley's Cup four times.

Turk was a character; I was fortunate enough to develop a relationship with him later in life.

Hockey wasn't my only focus growing up, however. I was extremely competitive in nature, so I was a multi-sports athlete, engaging in baseball, lacrosse, basketball, and hockey, of course, as well as any other pastime I could get my hands on in a pick-up game. I had plenty of friends and most of them were athletes, so finding something to do that involved competition, a winner and a loser, was never far away.

My brother, on the other hand, was a couple of years younger than I am so he had his own crew that he hung out with recreationally. He was still my baby brother and so pushing his buttons, utilizing some exasperating antics, were a part of my game; a part that came naturally. For instance, I remember waking him up at 1–2AM five Sundays in a row for Mass. He never took too kindly to that.

The incidences were run-of-the-mill for us. All in all, we had a good relationship; he was a great kid. He was the scholar in the family, but a good athlete as well.

Because of the slight age disparity, we faced off sparingly in organized leagues until we crossed paths one year in a lacrosse game. I was playing for Port Dalhousie and my brother was a member of the St. Catharines squad.

My mother was at the game and witnessed me pulling a couple of suspect maneuvers on my brother; maneuvers a ref would likely deem illegal had I been caught. My brother laughed it off; he had a sense of humor. Mom, however, wasn't too happy. She didn't talk to me for a couple of days, and only after she expressed her detest for what I did! That's how I played. I was aggressive and I wanted to win, even if it meant stepping on my brother's foot to get ahead during a lacrosse game.

In the end, none of that lacrosse stuff mattered. It was my dream to play professional hockey, and especially to play for the Toronto Maple Leafs. I knew that if I were to don the Leafs' colors as a hockey player someday, I'd have to do it one league at a time.

We didn't have school hockey growing up, so playing in an organized fashion meant suiting up for a CYO team and the Little NHL.

The Little NHL was formed by my father and a gentleman named Hall Judd. It was a league that began in St. Catharines, but due to a rapid expansion, would eventually stretch across Ontario.

Guys like Porky Douglas, Redd Reynolds, Cy Creswell, Billy Buschlin, Paddy Sherritt, and Bobby Twaddle all came on board as coaches to get things started. These men sacrificed a lot to ensure the kids got everything they could out of the league. As more and more kids joined, a younger crop of players would be added to the league.

I was conflicted though. I wanted to play for the city team, the St. Catharines Bantams, a traveling team that would play all over Ontario. I couldn't play both, but playing in the Little NHL was what my dad really supported. We got into it a few times. In the end, I played for the Bantams.

We had high hopes with good reason. My Bantam team was stout. We were coached by a legend in Vic Teal. Teal coached a juvenile team that won eleven All-Ontario Championships in a row with players like Stan Mikita, Elmer Vasko, and several others who went on to have great careers in the NHL.

Vic was a fundamentalist. He taught us how to skate, shoot, pass, and take the body; you name it. He was a hard-nosed guy who knew the game of hockey. If he was teaching skating drills, we couldn't fall. He wouldn't let us. If we did, we'd pay the price. I never complained. I got a lot out of Vic Teal's instruction.

He taught me a lot about the game. To say Vic Teal was a major influence in my life as a hockey player would be a gross understatement. Moreover, I firmly believe had I never been coached by Teal, I never would have made it to the NHL. He was that good. And what made him even more special was the fact that he did it all "pro bono," as a volunteer. His heart was in hockey, and it showed in his teaching.

As I formerly mentioned, we had a bunch of guys on that Bantam club who would eventually play in the NHL, two of which are in the Hall of Fame, me included. There was me, Ray Cullen, Jack Martin, Dougie Robinson, and Stan Mikita. Mikita was the other Hall of Famer on the team. He played his entire illustrious professional career with the Chicago Blackhawks and was considered one of the best centers in hockey during the 1960s.

However, the road to glory wasn't exactly paved on a shiny, velvety surface. We practiced before school at 6AM, three times a week. My parents dropped me off, picked me up, brought me home to shower, and it was off to class. But the hard work paid off. My Bantam team would face off in the All-Ontario Championship with the Toronto Marlies in consecutive seasons and win each time.

I had won championships early on in my hockey career, but nothing compared to this.

We played in some epic contests with the Marlies despite the fact we were overwhelming underdogs at the time. Argument being, the Marlies came from Toronto, a city back in the 50s and 60s with a population of about two million people, so they had a lot of quality hockey players to choose from. St. Catharines inhabited around thirty thousand, a bit less.

One year in the finals we traveled to Toronto and skated to a tie against the Marlies. We came back home and played in front of a sold-out St. Catharines Arena that held a raucous crowd of 3,200 folks at the time. We beat the Marlies 2–0 and won our first championship. The following year we beat them again.

Winning a pair of All-Ontario Championships in as many years was an aberration our team and the rest of St. Catharines would proudly accept. Looking back, I'd have to say those two championship seasons were my fondest memories as a kid.

But no matter how many games I played, won or lost, I always looked forward to taking a break from hockey. When the warm weather rolled around, myself, and the rest of the youth population of Canada would put the hockey equipment away in the corner of the basement or garage, and break out the lacrosse and baseball gear.

Contrary to popular belief, kids in Canada never played hockey twelve months a year. In fact, we were taught to "chill" in an effort to clear the mind and avoid burning ourselves out. Moreover, hockey is not Canada's sole national sport, it's actually only considered their national winter sport. It was declared in 1994 that lacrosse would become Canada's national summer sport. But for all intents and purposes, hockey is everything.

I'm not a believer in the notion that a kid needs to play hockey twelve months out of the year to continuously excel at it. A lot of parents in the United States instill such ideals that their kids should be skating all year round. However, a kid can develop skills in other sports such as baseball, lacrosse, and even soccer, which could increase their strength, flexibility, and range of motion, skills that no doubt will make him a better hockey player. An extended period of time away from the ice may even make him more eager to get back out there.

Nowadays, my favorite pastime, undisputedly, is golf. Truth be told, I don't think I swung a golf club more than five times as a kid. I never gave it a second thought when I was growing up in Canada.

So while hockey was number one in the frigid temperatures of winter, lacrosse and baseball took over the reigns in the summer; baseball, more so than lacrosse.

In fact, I remember a time when the Brooklyn Dodgers came to town and held a baseball camp for the kids. Stan Mikita and I were asked to try out for their Class D team, but we never went. I never had any aspirations of being a professional baseball player, nor did I believe I had the stuff to get there. I did, however, believe Stan could have made it. He was a wonderful baseball player and a natural athlete. Of course, we both made the right choice in not pursuing baseball, as we're now proud members of the Hockey Hall of Fame.

As much as we loved baseball and lacrosse, even in the summer we hit a point when we kids couldn't wait for the leaves to change colors as we'd once again crave putting the pads on and skating on the ponds. That was the emotion of most youngsters from the farm lands of the west and to the industrial cities of the east. Hockey was it, and it was always our first love.

Times have changed, I'm sure. The excitement is certainly there. You don't have to go further than understanding that 90 percent of the television sets in Canada tuned in to watch the gold medal game against the United States in the 2010 Olympics. But with respect to the kids and their "off seasons," I think nowadays they play more hockey year round than when I was a kid. I was never a big fan of that.

When we weren't playing hockey, winning championships, or participating in other sports, we found the time to let loose like most young kids would. Our days began at dawn; we'd go to school, and after school we'd play hockey until dinner time. Once feeding time was over, well, there were those instances where I had to fight that bored feeling. One Sunday evening, I impetuously decided to cure those jaded emotions. A score of my teammates and I felt compelled to check out a nudist camp near Fonthill, Ontario.

It was cold; so cold the camp dwellers were donning robes as they enjoyed their wiener roast on that brisk evening. Unfortunately, we didn't see anything worth mentioning. However, the nudist folks did. We got caught, and held in the police station where we'd be detained until our lacrosse coach came to bail us out.

My lacrosse coach, Joe McCafferey, got a big kick out of the situation, but would only say to us, "You guys couldn't steal shit from a chicken coop." He took it for what it was, though—a bunch of kids, harmlessly being, well, kids. Joe would eventually become the mayor of my city.

The story made the papers with names omitted, thankfully.

At the time of the incident, my dad had gotten in a bad car accident (hit by a train) and was laid up in the hospital for some time. Upon visiting him during his laborious stay, he was reading a story in the local paper about a bunch of kids from St. Catharines getting in trouble at a nudist colony in Fonthill. Dad went on a rant about how ungrateful these kids were, considering how much he'd done for them. In an effort to maintain a sturdy cover-up, I just agreed with him. In essence, I played 'mickey the dunce.'

The approach worked with dad, but with mom, not so much. She knew what happened because I was driving her car that night. But I'd get a reprieve from my mother. She protected me from dad.

Back on the ice, I had more pressing matters going on.

The Leafs began recruiting for their junior teams when I finished up with the St. Catharines, ON, Little NHL. Oddly enough, it was the wish of my parents for me to attend Notre Dame Secondary School in Toronto. The school was known less for its hockey, and more for its rowing, but I was active, and gung ho to win at something, so I wanted to go out for the rowing team. My dad protested; urged me to not row as the muscles working with the oars were drastically dissimilar from the muscles used as a hockey player.

I opposed his theory. To my eye, it seemed like a great idea. Conversely, after just a couple of practices, I was ready to listen. I couldn't get over how rigorous and intense the workouts were. I was done.

The school fielded a stout football program, but I wasn't going anywhere near that. I decided to hang up the paddles and continue to move forward playing hockey… somewhere.

Dad made the "somewhere" a little easier for me. He was the Assistant Manager of the St. Catharines Arena, the same facility the Toronto Maple Leafs trained in. The organization approached him after gaining interest in me as goaltender in my bantam days. The Leafs offered him a position as an Area Scout with the organization, and dad merrily accepted. I don't believe he lasted very long, though, as I was the only player he ever scouted.

Finding my way onto Toronto's doorstep was unconventional to say the least. No other kids that I knew of had a father who was a scout for an NHL team. But I didn't care. I had a secure pipeline that led straight to the Promised Land.

When all was said and done, the Leafs locked in on acquiring a commitment from me and a fellow named Jack Raymond Martin.

Martin was widely recognized as perhaps the greatest hockey player ever to come out of St. Catharines. He was a teammate of mine in bantam and played major roles in helping us win consecutive titles against our cross-territory foes, the Toronto Marlies.

Despite dad being a scout for the Leafs, Toronto didn't have to go very far to scout Jack or me. The recruiting system back in the day was based on territory, and though I hailed from the Chicago Blackhawks' region, the Maple Leafs could take two kids per year from the area if those recruits wanted to go to St. Mike's. In the end, the Leafs got what they wanted—commitments from both Jack and me.

So eventually I was to play for the St. Michaels Majors of the Ontario Hockey League (OHL). The Majors were the Maple Leafs' farm team affiliate, so if I had dreams of playing in Maple Leafs Gardens as a professional, this was the place to be. The OHL was a great league. Each team produced at least three to four hockey players yearly who would eventually go on to play in the NHL.

My dad's line of sight saw it as a perfect fit. But I didn't gaze upon things clearly; not as clearly as he did. I would have been happier, I thought, playing for the local team, the St. Catharines Teepees, and finishing out my teen years on the ice closer to home.

The Teepees were an Ontario Hockey Association club as well, but an affiliate of the Chicago Blackhawks.

I grew up watching the Teepees; I considered them iconic figures on the ice as a kid. As irony would have it, in 1954 the Teepees actually beat St. Michaels in a classic 8-game series to win the Memorial Cup as Canada's junior champion.

But my dad didn't want to hear any of it. He saw it differently, and any attempt to thwart his decision fell on deaf ears. Dad's house, dad's rules; I was going to St. Michaels.

Though the talk surrounding my future was largely based on hockey, school always came first. At the same time, however, the thought of ever becoming a doctor, lawyer, cop, or fireman never crossed my mind. The only thing that did was to be a professional hockey player. But that was, in all probability, 95 percent of a typical young boy's thought process in Canada. It was the Canadian dream. In my area, first came the Teepees, Junior A, and then it was on to the NHL. If you grew up in Ontario, that likely meant the Leafs.

I often wonder, even today, how dissimilar my life may have been had I maintained the line in the sand between my father and I. What would my life have been like if I had played for the Teepees instead of the Majors?

All I can do now is speculate. In the end I made a move, one that would prove to be advantageous on many levels.

ST. MIKE'S

I packed my bags, offered a farewell to my family and friends, and hoofed it to Toronto to play for the Majors.

I was there on scholarship. The Toronto Maple Leafs paid for my schooling and hockey, and gave me twenty dollars a week for laundry and odds and ends. For that, I'd be their goaltender.

The St. Michaels Majors were one of two junior hockey teams for the Toronto Maple Leafs in the Ontario Hockey League; the other being the Toronto Marlies. Non-Catholics were recruited to play for the Marlies, but the Catholics were made to play for the Majors.

Perhaps just as significant to point out, these esteemed hockey outfits possessed conflicting façades. St. Mike's was a high school, not a university. The Toronto Marlies were not. They were a junior hockey club affiliated with the Maple Leafs.

I had little idea of what to expect till the day I stepped foot on campus. I knew it was an all-boys school, something I had a difficult time preparing for. I knew it would be strict, and I would be managed by an array of authority figures at close quarters.

Moreover, this would be the first time in my life I'd be living a good distance from St. Catharines, away from my family and my closest friends. It was overwhelming, and to some extent, intimidating. Toronto was a major metropolitan city, and calling it home would take some getting used to. However, first, I'd have to wet my feet on campus before roaming the streets of the big city.

There were two houses on campus—Tweedsmere House (where I lived) and St. Claire House.

Tweedsmere was an old, eerily subdued mansion, standing three stories with each one housing a Prefect, or priest, who was in charge of a floor.

My first year on campus I would live on the third floor and my roommate was a fellow named Joe Verhoven. Joe wasn't a hockey player, but that wasn't uncommon. A lot of athletes were paired up with non hockey players; local guys with 'not-so-local guys' and so on.

The Verhoven clan hailed from Simcoe, ON, which was where they made their mark with the family business: tobacco growing.

Back at school we'd be in class from 8:20AM–3:20PM, dressed in a shirt and tie, blue blazer, and gray flannels. The rooms were small, giving way to twenty or thirty students or so. Our classes were anything but extraordinary, except we had to take a religion course, being that St. Mike's was a Catholic school.

The school moved forward stringently. If I had the sniffles there would be a horde of people taking care of me so I wouldn't miss significant class time, and to ensure I wasn't trying to dodge any of it either.

When the bell rang at the end of the day, what happened next depended on the time of year. Hockey didn't start for a couple of months from the time I settled on campus, so the kids found other ways to maintain their competitive belligerence, which included playing House League Football.

Today, you'd more than likely identify House League with intramural sports in colleges and universities. It worked out well for me because St. Mike's didn't allow me to play organized football. So I got behind center and called myself the quarterback. I was pretty decent, but House League was nothing like playing for the school. I could have gotten myself killed. During one game only three guys touched the ball: the center, halfback, and me. We were faintly predictable that particular day.

So, a few rigorous games of touch football, then hockey was upon us.

All levels of hockey in that day played under the umbrella of the Toronto Hockey League from bantam all the way up to Junior B, if you were lucky enough to get that far. I was fortunate enough to play with a number of guys who went through the system along with me, and several of those individuals were teammates of mine on Midgets for St. Mike's.

Practice was practice, but getting there was something else. St. Mike's didn't have its own arena so we were all over the place. After class we'd grab our equipment, travel by way of street, car, or bus for about an hour just to get to a rink. We were afforded a late dinner upon our return to campus. With any luck, we'd get our homework done and be ready to do it all over again the following day—unless it was a game night, in which case the day would stretch onward a bit longer.

Our first game as Midgets was against Shelton's Grocery Market of Stouffville, ON; they beat us. Just like that, we were sent down to play for the Minor Midget squad where we'd finish out the season.

Though we lost to a team that was more recognized for its exceptional produce in our inaugural contest, our team had a number of hockey players who would eventually skate in the NHL or with the Canadian national hockey team. Guys like Dave and Bruce Draper, Larry Keenan, Arnie Brown, Terry O'Malley, and Paul Jackson.

The talent on that team would make its mark as we would win the Minor Midget Championship our first season. We'd beaten mostly teams from suburban cities like Woodbridge, Leaside, Weston, and of course, the Marlies.

Our coach, David Bauer, was actually a priest at St. Mike's. A mere legend back in the day, he would become a major player in Canada's international hockey exploits. He racked up many career achievements, including winning the Olympic bronze for Canada as the Coach and General Manager in 1968. Bauer was a major influence in hockey and deserved much of the credit in winning it all that first season.

And it was a long season, so the school allowed all the kids off from Friday through Sunday to let loose a bit and experience what the city of Toronto had to offer. But this was only before and after the season—not during. However, when they came around, the long weekends on and off campus were helpful in my adjustment into this new environment.

During the first year we were expected to get a feel for the areas surrounding campus and get to know the other guys. And winning a championship made it that much better.

During that first summer off from St. Mike's, nothing wavered from the norm; I continued hanging out with Ray Cullen and Heber Crewe, played baseball and lacrosse, and all while taking a break from hockey.

The following year was much of the same, only this time I was at ease with my situation and would no longer have the need to acclimate myself to new surroundings. I had a solid group of friends coming back who lived on campus. But now I'd have a new roommate. His name was Bobby Adamo.

Bobby was a hockey player from Thunder Bay, Ontario. We played Junior B together later on. He was a good hockey player, though he never made it to the NHL.

In year two I met some good priests. Father Fallon, Father Neil Smith, and Father Volpe were all good guys and played key roles in student development.

That year I'd be bumped up to Junior B, along with several of the guys from the Minor Midget club that won it all the prior season. Father Bauer didn't particularly fancy the idea that he lost the core of his championship team from the previous year, but these things happened. He had visions of that club sticking together and winning multiple titles.

Junior B was a twenty and under league, so it was major jump from Minor Midget, and it showed in our play. We struggled.

But the following year reflected something else. Our core players returned, and once again we were led by Father Flanagan.

Despite falling short of any particle of success the previous year, we did develop some chemistry, a cohesiveness that would pay dividends that season.

As such, we clicked on all cylinders, choreographing our way to the championship round.

The finals brought an epic struggle that went seven games between us and the Dixie Beehives of Weston, Ontario.

The Beehives were another organization that would eventually produce a number of future NHL hockey players like David Burrows, Dave Poulin, Brendan Shannahan, and Denis DeJordy.

DeJordy was a sound goaltender for many years in the NHL, but before he collected game checks, he was the Beehives' starting net minder, and my counterpart that year in Junior B.

We beat DeJordy and the Beehives in game seven at Ted Reeve Arena in Toronto. I remember it vividly.

The arena filled up early with so many spectators I had a difficult time getting to the locker room to the point of near tardiness for warm-ups.

I had driven around the parking lot several times before I finally saw a parking spot. I made it, suited up, and would later relish the victory with my teammates.

After wrapping up the Metro B championship, it was thought by me and the rest of the guys that we had paved a road to compete for the Ontario Championship. However, the school sneered at the idea of extending an already pressure-packed campaign, and decided to pull the plug on our quest. The masses had come to the conclusion it was too much hockey—and academics would move to the forefront.

In the interim, I'd face everyday realities of high school life between my studies and everything else St. Mike's had to offer—like sock hops.

It was one of the oldest American high school traditions, and it was pretty popular in Canada as well. Most of the time it was fun, it came and went without any shenanigans. But the prom was different.

Jack Martin and I had worked the coatroom one year as the seniors enjoyed their final waltz in the St. Mike's gymnasium. It was a rather uneventful night for the elder kids, more so than they would have liked. About half the coats checked in had harbored some sort of alcoholic beverage, and each one had passed through Jack and me. It wasn't a favorable scenario for the jubilant partygoers, but it was for us. We swiped the liquor and had a grand old time disposing of it. The seniors were hopping mad, but nothing ever came of it. Unless we switched up a few coats and gave them to the wrong people, no one ever informed us of what we had done.

My social life at the school improved with every passing year; my friends and I would venture out to Toronto to escape the humdrum of our campus.

And though I whooped it up with my St. Mike's cohorts, my two closest buddies, still, were a couple of guys from St. Catharines, Ray Cullen and Heber Crewe. I would hang out with them during the summer months. I was about seventeen years old when I discovered pool halls. The three of us would play a lot of snooker, drink beers, and just hang out.

Whether it was a phony driver's license or someone else's birth certificate, we found ways to have a drink or two, responsibly, of course. None of us kids ever got out of hand.

About six of us rented a hotel room one time to set up a poker game and drink gin all night. It was a long evening. We dealt a lot of hands and downed a lot of shots. So many, the thought of ever having another sip of gin would never enter my thought process again. And it wouldn't surprise me if the other guys felt the same way.

There were those nights I'd craftily leave campus late into the evening to play penny Hearts with the crew from Supreme Cleaners, a dry cleaning business down the street from the campus. I'd play all hours of the night. It was harmless. It wasn't a particularly daring exploit, considering some of the other precarious activities I began to delve into.

A pal of mine, John Chasczewski, and I, decided to cover bets on the Kentucky Derby. The race was fast approaching, so we enlightened just a few of our house mates as they would become our first customers, and then made up our own odds—maybe the worst odds in the history of sports betting.

But despite the dubious probabilities handed out, we continued to attract clients. For two weeks we stealthily moved around campus with a list documenting everyone's wagers. Most bets ranged between $5 and $10. It didn't sound like much, but the influx of customers influenced the operation in another direction; it was out of hand.

On the eve of the race I had been called to the principal's office where I'd sit down with Father Reagan. He was a strict guy and commanded respect. I didn't know what to expect, but the hopes of leaving his office unscathed from a disciplinary standpoint seemed doubtful. I was ready to accept the news I'd be kicked out of school for turning the St. Mike's campus into a thriving gambling operation. I'd have to move home with nothing more than a few good memories and an 'almost made it' tag on my back.

I waited for a few minutes outside the office, but it felt like hours before the secretary finally signaled to me that it was time to sit down with Father Reagan. I walked in and was greeted with a stern order to sit down. I did, swiftly. He looked me grimly in the eye and asked, "What are the odds on Tim Tam?"

I said, "3–1, Father, but I'll give you 4–1."

He asked, "Can you put $10 on him to win?"

Without hesitation I assured him the bet was in, and that was that. I walked out of the office with my body puffing out an enormous sigh of relief.

The race came and went melodramatically. However, after being introduced to the prospect of being kicked out of school so unceremoniously, I decided to retire, and my reign as bookmaker ended at the finish line that year.

The near expulsion wasn't the only heart pounding experience for me as a teen. The other was in 1957, the year I met my future wife, Betty Sciamonte, an employee of my mom's at the Real Estate Board in St. Catharines.

She was a true beauty, kind and warm hearted.

Betty grew up three streets away, but strangely enough, I never knew she existed until one evening when my brother asked if I'd give him and a few of his classmates a ride to a high school dance. At the end of the night I picked up my brother along with Betty and her cousin. We hung out at the beach, had a wonderful time together that night, and the rest is history.

When the summer arrived, once again, I'd pick up where I left off the year before, playing baseball and lacrosse. And when the latter end of the warm weather was upon me, I'd get ready for another season on the ice at St. Mike's. Only this time I'd be playing Junior A.

I had been called up once before to play in a Junior A game. I was giddy. My dad bought me a flat top hat that I sported on my way to the game. But the blissful beginning to the day ended with tragedy in the wee hours of the night.

My grandfather, Jim Cheevers, was a traveling salesman and had decided to come to the game. He was a proud man, and overjoyed knowing all I had accomplished to that point in my life. But that evening, after the game, he passed away in his sleep.

When I reached Junior A, I was in awe. It was a wonderful time. Every Sunday we'd play at home in the Maple Leafs Gardens in front of upward of 16,000 fans. We were part of a double header with the Toronto Marlies, the other host. It was a remarkable experience. Sunday hockey was it back then.

At the end of my first year in Junior A we lost to my hometown Teepees in the finals in the Ontario Championship. They had a wealth of talent over there, including some future NHL hockey players like Ray Cullen, Vic Hadfield, Whitey Stapleton, and an outstanding goaltender by the name of Roger Crozier. It was a good year, but we fell short.

That first season was an eye opener, and if I learned one thing, it was this: making the jump to Junior A was a big deal. The talent level was vastly superior to Junior B. A lot of guys I played with my first year at St. Mike's never made it that far. Only the elite that St. Mike's had to offer would play at that level. I was now on the doorstep of playing professional hockey.

The school always put academics first and athletics second. Without the grades, there would be no hockey. But with my eyes focused on getting to the NHL, my studies would now warm on the back burner for good. Though my text books would see less action, I'd never put myself in a position where my eligibility to play hockey would be called into question.

My second year in Junior A, which was my last, I was the standby goalie for the Maple Leafs and the visiting team. Now I'd be getting paid.

In those days NHL teams only carried one goalie, so as the standby I'd be available for the Maple Leafs' absent goaltender or the opposing team's net minder, lest one of them got hurt. And I did it all for $10 a game. It wasn't a large amount, even back then, but if I suited up for eight or nine games in a month, it would add up.

In the meantime, St. Mike's was clicking on all cylinders all the way to the Memorial Cup once again. The finals were played in Edmonton. We boarded Air Canada and dashed cross country.

A lot of the guys were nervous; 99 percent of them had probably never flown on a plane before. I wasn't fazed much. I'd read, fall asleep, wake up, and read again. Once we landed, things didn't get any better. We'd play in one of the more unfriendly venues for a visiting hockey team. Nonetheless, we won the series 4–2 and once again, St. Mike's could raise another championship banner.

Winning the Memorial Cup was a big deal. The closest comparison I can render would be that of winning the BCS Championship in college football.

The series attracted plenty of fans and local media, and college scouts from around North America. It was there in Edmonton where I met a man named Murray Armstrong, the head coach of the University of Denver in Colorado.

I developed a good rapport with Murray, and as a result of our communications I was enticed enough to explore the idea of going to college in the United States. I applied to the University of Denver and was accepted.

My bags were all but packed until I received a phone call late that summer from an individual representing the Maple Leafs. He told me, in no uncertain terms, I was the property of Toronto and thus I would not be afforded an opportunity to attend college or play hockey elsewhere— unless it was for the Leaf's organization.

Before the phone call I thought I was in the clear. To that point in my career, for whatever reason, I hadn't signed a C-Form. The C-Form was a binding agreement between an amateur hockey player and an NHL team. Once the prospect signs, the rights of his eligibility to play professional hockey is owned by that organization. However, I had not signed the C-Form with respect to me playing college hockey. And it had never come up in conversation. Unknowingly, I had become a professional hockey player. I played Junior A and I got paid for it. However, the $10 I received each game as a stand-bye was not allowed in the eyes of the NCAA. And since the Leafs had the check stubs to prove it, I had no leg to stand on. Had I met Murray Armstrong two years prior, as a Junior B player, I might have stood on higher ground. I would have boarded the next bus to Denver, Colorado.

With thoughts of playing collegiate hockey becoming all but a distant memory, my thinking would now move to the fore; to life after St. Mike's. Father Bauer negotiated my first professional contract with Toronto. I would be given a $3,000 signing bonus, which in those days was a hefty sum for playing hockey. My salary would be $5,000 my first season and $5,500 in year two.

There was nothing in my way now. I was strong, healthy, and I never missed any playing time. It wasn't until my last year of Junior A when St. Mike's needed to prepare for my departure. They did so by playing a younger goaltender in my place by the name of Dave Dryden.

Dryden's commitment to playing for St. Mike's depended on him playing in twelve games in my place in Junior A. Father Bauer agreed, then pulled me aside to keep me apprised of the situation. I'd be playing forward now for a dozen games. I thought he was nuts, and I told him so. I was an all-star goalie, my argument was. But he insisted it would be good for me.

Not only was it good for me, but it was good for the rest of the league.

I was an aggressive goaltender. I swung my stick a lot and irritated a lot of guys on opposing teams. This was their chance to get even. I'd go in the corner to dig a puck out and I'd be met by a party of five every time. I never scored a goal, but I recorded a couple of assists here and there. I had one golden opportunity—a breakaway once. I was alone. In front of me was Roger Crozier of St. Catharines. I always thought I'd know what to do on a breakaway because of my experiences on the other end as a goaltender. I thought wrong. From twenty feet out, I snapped a "wrister" into Crozier's chest. Suffice it to say, it was the toughest stint in my young career. But I got through it.

As far as injuries went at St. Mike's, the lone scratch would come from a target-finding puck that met and broke my cheekbone during a playoff game as a goaltender. However, I wasn't cut and my teeth remained intact. I put some ice on it. It healed on its own, and I went back out there and played.

It wasn't until my last couple of years at St. Mike's that we were given masks to wear. It was around that time when the goalie mask was introduced in hockey. I wore mine in practice. It was heavy; it stuck to my face and it fogged up something terrible in a matter of minutes. It didn't make sense. The mask goaltenders use today makes sense. It's there for protection and it works. Every game we see pucks deflecting off a goalie's mask that would otherwise do some real damage to a person's face.

For the time being, I was a fan of a mask.

When all was said and done, I always regarded St. Mike's as a special place for me. I made a lot of friends and forged many bonds. Over the years, however, it became increasingly difficult to keep in touch when so many of us went our separate ways. Some continued to play hockey, some did not. Others would simply fade away.

But the remembrance of St. Mike's would follow me everywhere. Oftentimes when I was firmly ensconced as an NHL goaltender, individuals would approach me, introduce themselves, and begin speaking about the old days. I didn't always remember their names, or any experiences I may have had with them. But I did remember where I last saw them—it was at St. Mike's.

GOING PRO

With juniors winding down, I began to look forward to the next step in my career. College was now out due to a technicality, so if I had an eye on continuing to play hockey in my abrupt future, it would be as a professional for the Toronto Maple Leafs.

In the summer of '61 I turned pro.

With my finances taking a blatant turn for the better, I decided to dowry myself with something special. I purchased my first car—a '57 Chevy.

It was a great time in my life. I had my new ride and the prospects of a lengthy, thriving professional hockey career.

In those days, gearing up to play at the pro level was a little atypical compared to what players experience today. I maintained my competitive edge by continuing to play lacrosse in the warm weather months versus hitting the weights, but this time I needed to embrace an off-road activity to prime myself as an NHL goaltender.

In the spirit of exertion, Jack Martin and I would visit a local high school where we could jump on the track and run a few laps. So that's what we did. We toured the rubber a couple times beginning at roughly 11:55AM, and capped off the routine with ten or twelve beers at around 12PM at a local bar, just when the bars began opening in the area. Our timing was impeccable.

When training camp opened, the first order of business was to take a physical. Unfortunately, for me, it was the natural order of things for any professional sports organization. The line was typically formed by alphabetical order, and one year, just ahead of me, and on his way to the platform, was a fellow named Wayne Carlton.

Wayne had a body like the Greek god Zeus; he looked like he was chiseled from stone. My physique was a little less spectacular, so I felt a certain level of indignity as my turn approached. However, the uneasiness of the situation would take a back seat when Wayne astoundingly failed the physical. Even more surprising was that I passed! It was an ancillary step on the way to becoming a pro for Wayne. He eventually did pass and endured a professional career spanning many years.

When the screening phase mercifully concluded that first year, it was time to play hockey. I remember being in the goalie's room along with two other net minders, Johnny Bower and Terry Sawchuk. They were a couple of great hockey players and future Hall of Fame guys. It was surreal to be rubbing shoulders with these guys, in the same locker room. I knew I was where I wanted to be.

The daily life of a professional hockey player was, of course, nothing I'd ever experienced, so it was a bit of a culture shock. If I could point out a glaring similarity between juniors and the pros, it was the fact that I always had the opportunity to covertly veer off the reservation and have some fun before and after curfew. If I could point out a glaring difference, it was the overall treatment and amenities afforded to us as professionals. Everything was great in Junior A, but in the pros it's first class all the way.

We ditched the buses for planes and trains, and the food was quality. I would embrace the lavishness with glee.

But no matter how groovy things appeared on the surface, I was still struggling to acclimate to a new lifestyle.

The team practiced hard, twice a day, and had to walk to the rink just to get there. And I did. I never faltered.

Our first exhibition contest was in Niagara Falls against the Boston Bruins. A few days prior I had taken my plastic mask off in practice because it was fogging up and affecting my vision. Of course, the second shot I faced in the scrimmage game whacked me off my forehead, splitting me open, and leaving me with an eight-inch gash just below my hairline. But I didn't care, honestly. No one wore a mask back then, so I hardly felt regret, just a little pain as the blood cascaded down my face.

I was having a good training camp, and the coaching staff alerted me to that fact. They felt I had promise. I had potential, but no team to play for. Bower and Sawchuk were firmly planted on the roster, and the Leafs weren't going to carry three goaltenders. There were options, though. The organization's farm team was the Rochester Americans, so in the event a spot opened up for the minor league club, I could stake a claim to it. However, in the short term, I stayed with the Leafs during camp, practicing, even accompanying the team on their west coast exhibition tour.

It was a lot of fun out there with guys like Eddie Shack and Tim Horton. Shack and I roomed for a period of time. He was a character. His nickname was "The Entertainer." I don't want to say we snuck out from time to time, but we did find ourselves away from our accommodations and the Leafs' coaching staff, late night, on a few occasions.

One particular night at the end of training camp, and much to my surprise, Johnny Bower, who was my roommate at the time, took me out for a beer and steak. It was astounding to me, because he never had a reputation for throwing the bucks around. When I asked what the occasion was, he said he'd signed a three-year contract and that he would be set for life. When I asked him how much he would be making, he replied with, "I'll make $10,000 this year, $11,000 next year, and $13,000 the year after next."

I said, "Oh, you are set for life."

And he was. That was good money at the time.

Dickie Moore was one of the older veterans on the team that taught me the ropes and would become a great influence on me during the infant stages of my career. I spent a lot of time with him on and off the ice and always relished my experiences with him.

During the season, if I was ever to feel the slightest bit of apprehension, I was fortunate to have been a teammate of Bert Olmstead.

Bert was a great hockey player and, like Dickie, was a seasoned veteran. He took me under his wing and really showed me what being a professional hockey player was all about. No one worked harder than Bert. He knew it, and wanted me to follow his example. Bert kept a close eye and made sure I put the work in.

Now, though I was secure in the fact I could play in this league, my playing time would remain in limbo until I was notified I'd be heading over to play for the Sault Ste. Marie Thunderbirds, an organization in the Eastern Professional Hockey League and affiliate of the Chicago Blackhawks.

That was the climate in hockey during that era. Players were lent all over the place until they found a permanent home on a club, or got sent home for good. So, instead of skating with Rochester, I crossed over and played in another league with a different organization.

That season a couple of hot young prospects from the Chicago Blackhawks organization came over to play with us at the tale of the year, one of which was Phil Esposito. Phil was, in fact, a native of Sault Ste. Marie.

It was a bittersweet time in my life. Playing hockey was all I wanted to do, but the everyday life changes had an air of glum from time to time.

This would be my first Christmas away from home, and it hurt. When the holiday season approached I decided to do something special for my mom. I completed a color-by-number painting of horses for her that took me a month or better to complete. Frankly, it was a proud moment for me. She loved horses, so I couldn't wait to give it to her. But a dark cloud loomed over my magnum opus in the form of a widowed lady who I was renting a room from in her house. She was cleaning one day and unconsciously dusted my ponies, turning my once masterwork painting into a smudge farm. Needless to say, it was a difficult thing for me to swallow; all that hard work, and the anticipation of mom's gleeful acceptance of my gift was forever lost. It was of little consolation, but the widow felt my pain and cried along with me.

That season the Sault Ste. Marie Thunderbirds were coached by a man named John "Black Jack" Stewart. Jack, as most people called him, was a former defenseman for the Detroit Red Wings and Blackhawks. He was known for his toughness on the ice, and did little to shed his reputation of hardiness as a coach. He got on players routinely about their performance. I recall an instance when he heckled John Chasczewski, the same fellow I partnered up with in taking bets for the Kentucky Derby back at St. Mike's. John contended he couldn't play unless the team issued him new skates. Jack held nothing back in telling him, "I could do better myself in my shoes."

John said, "But you have new shoes."

Aside from being just another professional hockey club, Sault Ste. Marie had an identifying stain on them: They traveled by limousine. It was cheaper than packing the buses, and I can only assume it was for no other reason than the fact that one of the owners of the club owned a limousine company. We'd fit in the area of six or seven guys in a limo, hauling four limos all around the league from one arena to the next.

The lavishness in the way we traveled did little to help the team's performance on the ice though. We lost a lot of games that year, and each time we took the ice, there was a recurring sense to it all. The EPHL was only a four-team league, so needless to say, familiarity between the teams and individual players was an unremitting certainty. Getting from one opponent to the next took a little less than making sure the limo driver didn't doze off behind the wheel on the way.

Off the ice, things ran quite typical for me and the guys, for the most part. However, I did play a lot of pool up there in Sault Ste. Marie. I felt it one night, and brazenly accepted a game of snooker with Willy Hoppe, one of the world's most renowned billiards champions at the time. The outcome was somewhat foreseeable. The score was 100-0 in his favor, but there was a silver lining—I got to play with Willy Hoppe.

In the middle of the season I finally made my way over to Rochester where I played with guys like Jimmy Pappin, Billy "Hinky" Harris, and Dick Gamble. Harris and Gamble were a couple of old pros. Pappin, however, was a former opponent of mine when he was with the Toronto Marlies. Jimmy was a very good hockey player. He had spent several years in the Toronto organization until he later played with the Chicago Blackhawks.

It was good having Jimmy around. He was another face who was reminiscent of the days I spent at St. Mike's.

We lived outside Rochester in a place called Pittsford, and it was a lot of fun.

Conversely, the amusement had to change venues because before I knew it, the goalie for the American Hockey League's Pittsburgh Hornets got hurt. So the Leafs lent me over there where I'd play my first professional game. Ironically, in that first game we'd square off against Toronto's Rochester team and defeat the Americans 2–1.

It was a nice way to begin my career. But in the meantime, I had a lot to learn about being a professional goaltender, including what to expect from certain players across the league: the scorers, the "tough guys", and so on.

The Cleveland Barons had a hockey player named Freddy Glover. Freddy had a professional career as a player that extended twenty-eight years, primarily in the AHL, with a couple of short stints in the Chicago Blackhawks' and Detroit Red Wings' organizations. After he retired he coached for thirteen years at the AHL and NHL levels.

Freddy Glover was one of the toughest guys I'd ever seen in my life on skates. I remember vividly cranking him as he stood in front of the net. Being it was my first full year as a pro, it was a bold attempt at letting my presence be known as an AHL goaltender. Bold but brash, as the next thing I knew, I was cupping my forehead watching the blood coagulate down my face and onto the ice. He stuck me with the blade of his stick pretty good. It was payback, but more importantly, it served as a welcoming shot to the AHL, which was the toughest league going at the time, and I could regrettably attest to that.

Though I could say my indoctrination into professional hockey began with a few stitches above my brows, most days seldom ended without having a few laughs with the array of characters I played with.

Earl "Ching" Johnson was a career minor league journeyman and teammate of mine with Pittsburgh in the 1961–62 season. To the rest of the world he was better known for playing one regular season game with the Detroit Red Wings in 1953–54, and in unpredictable fashion, had his name engraved on the Stanley Cup after Detroit became champions that year. But to us, Ching was known as simply a guy who stuttered a lot.

Earl came down ill one day. He called another player, Dick Mattiussi, a hard-nosed, physical defenseman, to tell him he wasn't going to make it to practice that day. Ching stuttered, using his unambiguous, 6:1 syllable-to-word ratio when speaking, but failed to mention it was he who was calling. Dick responded by saying, "Thanks, Ching."

Ching stuttered, "How did you know it was me?"

It was apparent who the caller was, and we had a good laugh over it. And we had a lot of good laughs.

Along with finding good humor, I loved to learn. The fact I was always so keen on my new setting really made for a smooth transition for me into minor league hockey. So, whereas a lot of guys may have taken special measures to acclimate themselves to a novel domain, I had an easier time of it. And it got easier when I met a man named Normie Corcoran.

Normie was a teammate of mine, and one of Canada's greatest lacrosse players. My dad and Normie had known each other for some time, and had forged a long standing friendship. Normie had great admiration for my dad. So, suffice it to say, we hit it off right away.

Normie took me under his wing. He was a great hockey player, so I learned a lot from him on the ice. On our days off we'd hang out and have some beers or head to the races. If ever I demonstrated an ounce of nostalgia, it would usually be lost on the days I spent with Normie. Especially on a long bus trip, when killing time was on the front burner for all on board for any club I played on, including the Hornets.

Our Pittsburgh team was managed by a former professional goaltender named Baz Bastein, who had his career cut short in 1949 while playing for the Hornets. He took a puck in his right eye during training camp. The injury was so devastating his eye had to be removed, and replaced with a glass one.

On the road, we did what we could to avoid hours of sustained monotony. We often got a game of poker going and Baz happened to be one of our regular players. During one particular game, in the middle of a hand, Baz' glass eye fell out and rolled next to a guy's hand in the game. He was accused of cheating. But Baz wasn't cheating, and later, after the spat, we found humor in the story. We found humor in anything, though. We had to, to keep moving.

The AHL was a special place, and if I didn't know my place, I could be replaced. At that particular time, teams only carried one goalie. Typically, the trainer for each team was the backup in practice. So if the #1 guy got hurt, or couldn't play, a lot of times the guy who stitched you up the day before would throw the pads on and position himself between the pipes in a game that counted. In the meantime, an organization could call someone up from another team to fill in. I had nowhere to play, so when Pittsburgh's goalie got hurt, I got the call. That's how I ended up there.

When the regular season came to a close that year, I was back skating for Rochester.

That year, my old lacrosse team made it to the Man Cup, which was the Canadian Championship. I wanted to play in the series, but the Leafs forbade me. However, the series was to be played in Cornwall, Ontario, and Punch Imlack, the General Manager of the Maple Leafs at the time, used to play lacrosse in the festive town. I pled a good case and talked him into letting me play one game. Consequently, it had to come with a stipulation. I had to sign a waiver stating I was responsible for any injuries I may suffer during the game. I suffered none, and the team lost the series to New Westminster.

Nonetheless, when I left the locker room that year for the last time I headed home, only this time I would lack the desire to play lacrosse or baseball and decided to focus on training hard for hockey; all the while taking up a part-time job at the Fort Erie Race Track selling tickets in their mutual department. Every now and then I worked in the early mornings walking the horses.

The "Fort" had been in business since 1897. To this day, it's considered by many, including myself, to be one of the most beautifully constructed tracks in North America. I really enjoyed working there.

I began the 1962–63 season with Rochester playing in nineteen games, before I was moved down to the Sudbury Wolves in the EPHL. I was frustrated. From a personal standpoint, that particular season was marked by a loathsome feeling. It was the first time in my career I had second thoughts about playing professional hockey. I had begun to lament each time I was moved to a different team.

It was during a game against the Syracuse Braves when my thoughts of leaving the game transformed into something genuine. After a half-day ride to upstate New York, we found the ice in the arena to be nearly black. We couldn't see the puck. The score was 8–8 when I nearly packed it in emotionally.

I never took any sincere steps toward quitting the game at that point, but my thoughts ran in that direction for some time. In time, the downbeat mind-set eventually ran out of gas and I'd bounce back, and focus once again on a future in hockey. I suppose, given my love for the game, it was just a matter of time before I'd pull myself out of this funk.

After all, Sudbury was a fun place.

I lived on Ramsey Lake with a good group of guys, including Dave Richardson and Mike McMahon. We kept to ourselves for the most part, until the team decided we needed to expose an "all hands on deck" approach aimed at the organization.

It was that season that the Wolves had difficulty making payroll, and had reached a point when they couldn't pay us. They ran out of "cheese." When that moment arrived we went on strike. Truth be told, we took a desultory approach to the situation. It was just a few days, so we took the opportunity for a getaway. I went to Toronto with Gary Jarret and a few others. Some guys went skiing or found other creative ways to fill their time. I don't even think we missed any games; even Dave Richardson, whose tardiness on one account made for one heck of a tale, did not miss one game.

The strike was over, and the team was scheduled to play an inter-league game against the Fort Wayne Komets of Indiana out of the International Hockey League. We had to promptly catch the bus home after the game because we had an afternoon contest the very next day. It was a ten- to twelve-hour drive depending on the weather. Dave, however, missed the bus. But in an effort to get back, he hitchhiked, and beat us home! So Dave thumbed his way nearly 500 miles to get to a game; it must be some kind of record for the EPHL.

Our Sudbury team was coached by Erwin Grove "Murph" Chamberlain. Murph led a somewhat mercurial lifestyle, but as a coach, he was tough, and there were few better.

It was a train ride from Sudbury to St. Louis. I was ready for dinner. I sat down salivating over two chickens and six beers sitting in front of me. Murph always had a problem with my weight, so when he took notice of my little feast, he made his way over to me and said, "No wonder you're so friggin' fat." That was the extent of Murph's subtlety when referring to my weight. Quite honestly, the organization had a problem with the extra baggage I was carrying, and I was called in to do something about it, but it never went beyond that.

The club went to the finals that year and beat out a very good Montreal team. For some reason Murph Chamberlain-coached teams always faced off against the Canadiens' minor league affiliates and always gave them fits.

Murph was certainly a character, but we had a few eccentric personalities on the team as well, including a one Red Armstrong. Red loved to fight; he actually enjoyed it. He especially loved to fight during the last five minutes of the game—so he wouldn't have to sit in the penalty box.

The locker room to Red was what a phone booth was to Superman. No one dressed faster than he, the quickest I'd ever seen. He was a colorful guy.

That year Red got called up to the Leafs and on his first shift, he scored a goal in seven seconds. Everyone across Canada heard the goal as it was aired on Hockey Night in Canada. The following night he was involved in a fight outside Union Station waiting for us to come through there. The man just loved to brawl.

When the season ended I went back to my previously habitual pastime and played senior lacrosse over the summer, and continued working at the track. Fifty-five hundred dollars a year from the Maple Leafs was good, but I needed to save some money in the off-season as a safety net. I remember Red asking me if I was going to save any money one particular summer.

I told Red, "If I could save two that would be great. What about you, Red?" I asked.

"I'm going to save three," he said.

"Really?" I said, "You're going to save three thousand?"

"Oh, you're talking about thousands?"

Though Red's ambition for saving dough that summer lacked some vigor, he was a good guy and a good hockey player.

When the 1963–64 campaign opened, I had made the Rochester team as the starting goalie. There I'd meet Joe Crozier, the coach and manager of the team. Joe was another very influential character in my career. He was a great teacher, motivator, and a superb hockey guy.

And it was in Rochester that season when I'd first become acquainted with none other than Don "Grapes" Cherry. Don was a very good hockey player, and maybe the toughest defenseman I'd ever seen. He loved to fight, too. In fact, he loved it so much he studied the art of pugilism on ice. In doing so, Grapes was one of the best fighters in hockey. I remember him squaring off against Spider Mazur in Providence, which turned out to be one of the best fights I had ever witnessed in hockey. It was a physical game. Don and Spider went at it, sticking each other when they could until they both dropped the gloves and engaged in an epic battle. After the scrap they got stitched up in the same locker room and carried on like it never happened.

But moreover, Don Cherry was a skilled defenseman. Though he never had a great shot, he had a knack for scoring goals. He had great command of his stick and used his exceptional physicality to continuously gain great position. When Don was on the ice, I always saw the puck. He always had a way of making it easier for me out there.

Overall it was a fun season. I played with a lot of great guys and we spent a lot of time together off the ice. I lived in a house with Red, Larry Gordan, and the team's other goaltender, Eddie Babiuk. In fact, we lived in several dwellings that year because we kept getting kicked out. We'd sign a lease, and a month or two later, we'd be told we had to go. We liked to have fun, so if we weren't out amusing ourselves at our favorite watering hole, The Turf Bar, we would find something else to do at home. Unfortunately, that "something to do" usually ticked off the landlord.

Of course, we got the attention of management by engaging in some risqué activities away from hockey, so we had to sit through a few disciplinary meetings from time to time. Yet it was nothing that ever got out of control, at least the meetings never did!

We played well that year and won some games, but lost in the first round of the playoffs to the eventual Calder Cup champions, the Cleveland Barons.

In 1964, I began the season without a contract. In those days we never dealt with agents, so I was doing my own negotiating with the team's manager and coach, Joe Crozier. I wanted $6,500 for the year. The NHL minimum wasn't too far off at $7,500, so I was cutting it close. But Joe had an idea. He approached me and said, "I'll tell you what, I'll give you $100 a week, every week you lead the league in goals against average (GAA)."

I said, "Ok," and led the league each week from beginning to end, and consequently received a bonus of $2,600.

The 1964–65 season was a banner year for more reasons than just my eccentric contract. The team compiled 48 wins and took the AHL's Western Division. The number 48 was also significant, in that I started each game we won, thus setting a record for most wins by a goaltender in the American Hockey League. I started all 72 games and was named as an all-star representative.

We had a great coach in Crozier, and as a team we were talented and driven. A couple of our defensemen, Larry Hillman and Al Arbour, were first team all-stars, as were the forwards on our first line, Bronco Horvath, Gerry Ehman, and Stan Smrke. The second line had no slouches, either, showcasing Billy Harris, Dick Gamble, and Eddie Litzenberger. Most of the guys, in fact, played in the NHL at one time or another, so we had a good mix of young talent and veteran players.

When the playoffs began, we had good sense to be confident. We beat the Quebec Aces 4–1 in round one. It was a great win, but it may have been overshadowed by a big brawl during one of the games at their place. The series garnered so much attention due to the scuffle that the following day at practice the arena drew upward of ten thousand spectators.

At any rate, after earning a bye in round two, we faced off against the

Hershey Bears in the finals and would claim victory once again by a 4–1 margin, winning the Calder Cup for the first time in Rochester's history.

Up to that point in my career it was my fondest memory as a minor league hockey player. I had bounced around, and been lent here and there to different clubs. But during that particular season for the Americans, I played end to end as the starter with essentially the same group of core guys. It meant a lot winning that championship. It meant even more because my dad was there to witness the triumph.

After the game everyone on the team hit a bar in town called The Downtowner. We were having fun celebrating, drinking beers, and 'high-fiving' each other. My dad was in attendance and made his presence abundantly clear when he ordered champagne for everyone in honor of the victory. We got a lot out of that night, my dad and me. He got the nickname, Champagne Joe, and I got the bill.

My hometown was roughly three and a half hours away from the bar. My dad and his friends jumped on the highway, but drove three and a half hours in the opposite direction! Perhaps he ordered one too many bottles of the bubbly; however, thankfully, nearly eleven hours after the party ended, dad made it home safe.

When night became day, and spring became summer, an air of uncertainty had loomed over me. The Maple Leafs now had to protect me or place me on waivers, but only as a forward, since I played twelve games as a winger in juniors. That was the only way the team could retain me, because the organization had an eye on protecting their other two stud goaltenders, Bower and Sawchuk. So Punch Imlack tried to protect me as a forward, but the league wouldn't go for it. So it was just a matter of time before the uncertainty would morph into something certain; my days with Toronto were numbered.

I was working at the race track that summer when I got paged over the intercom by a guy who knew someone in the Toronto organization. This 'guy' informed me that Toronto was ready to protect me along with the two aforementioned goaltenders already under contract. But it never made sense to me. I walked out, picked up a paper, and learned in a most unexpected fashion that the Boston Bruins had acquired me via the waiver draft! I was visibly disgusted, and physically animated. After reading the news I gave the paper a "Pele-eske" kick. I wanted to be a Maple Leaf, and Boston was weak at the time. They were so weak I remember my friend reacting to the news by saying, "It's already 1-0."

But what Boston offered was something alternative, something bigger and "badder," something special. I just hadn't seen it yet.

ON TO BOSTON

During the 1920s the NHL consisted of ten teams, but the financial pressures brought on by the Great Depression and World War II caused four organizations to drop out. As a result, for a period of twenty-five years between 1942 and 1967, the league stood with six teams. Those clubs collectively would be named the "Original Six." The Boston Bruins were one of them.

Boston had a quasi resemblance to the Maple Leafs; they, too, already encompassed a rich hockey tradition. Yet I still felt great apprehension moving over to the Bruins. They were struggling to maintain consistency for a long period of time, and their developmental system was not coming along like they had hoped.

When training camp opened, I couldn't help but feel a twinge of ambiguity running through my mind as I began to take notice that I wasn't the only goaltender in town again! Now I was competing with Bernie Parent and Eddie Johnston. And like my previous competitors, Bower and Sawchuk, both Parent and Johnston were very talented.

Setting aside my discontent for the situation I was in, I did, however, find solace in the fact that it was a small league—and with that came some familiarity with players I had forged relationships with in the past. I bumped into Barry Ashbee, a Weston, Ontario, native. Ashbee was a former lacrosse opponent, but a member of the Boston Bruins organization at that time, and one of the toughest players in the NHL. Later in his career he was acquired by the Philadelphia Flyers. With his name synonymous with toughness, Barry would earn his place as part of the famed crew known as the "Broad Street Bullies."

We were staying in a hotel up in London, Ontario, during camp. As Barry and I walked the courtyard of the hotel one afternoon, we crossed paths with Leighton A. "Hap" Emms, the Bruins new General Manager. Hap was a player/coach/general manager/owner in hockey for nearly sixty years; he was a busy guy. So we were excited to meet him. Barry introduced himself, and it was at that moment when Hap turned to me and said, "I didn't get your name." Suffice it to say, the encounter with Hap did little to thwart my feeling of angst; in fact, it served as an indication, at least to me, that I had no chance with Hap.

Hap Emms was callous by nature and an incompetent leader. I remember an instance when I was called up to Boston from Oklahoma City. I was up at 6AM. I had to carry my equipment to the airport where I'd catch a plane to Chicago, change planes, pick up my equipment, and fly to Boston to arrive by 7PM that night. So I put in for one day's meal money, plus cabs in each location. I logged about $35 in expenses for the day, when Hap called me into his office. He handed me my expense check and said, "Here you go, but just so you know, we know you got a meal on the plane." I took the check, threw it back at him, and walked out. I didn't want it.

He had an appalling tendency to treat people like they were babies. I didn't care. I let most of his anger roll off my back, and when an opportunity presented itself to acerbate the taste in his mouth, I took it.

After a 9–2 beating handed down by the Montreal Canadiens one night, Hap approached me in front of the players and asked, "What happened out there?"

I said to Hap, "Roses are red, violets are blue. They got nine, and we got two."

Oddly, Hap's wife used to travel with him on road trips. The team had to endure not only the often irritable Mr. Emms, but his best lady, as well—until one night, on a bus ride back home from Montreal. Things quickly got ugly.

We had just lost to the Montreal Canadiens. A lot of the guys sat behind "Lady Emms" this time, and for most of the duration of this trip, the men had expressed enough indignity to make even the worst fellow think twice about accompanying the team on another bus ride. They were a bunch of dejected guys reacting to a tough loss to their division rivals. Needless to say, she'd had enough. That night would mark the end of the traveling Mrs. Emms.

Now, despite the stiff competition I would face at the goaltender's position that year, and the obvious lack of adoration between me and Hap Emms, I did start the season in Boston my rookie year with the Bruins.

Milt Schmidt was the head coach. He was a lifelong Bruin, playing sixteen years in the NHL, all with Boston. Schmidt was one of the all-time Bruins greats, helping the organization win two Stanley Cups in 1939 and 1941. He was a hard-nosed player who brought his gristly "on the ice" attitude to the bench.

That season, my counterpart, Eddie Johnston, was my first roommate. We spent a lot of time hanging out after practice, having a beer or two with the other guys. We hit it off right away. Eddie was a couple of years older than I was. He was a very good goaltender and had been with the organization since '62, so I learned a lot from him.

I got into just 7 games for Boston that season, and before I could warm up for number 8, I suffered a knee injury, forcing the organization to send me down to their minor league affiliate, the Oklahoma City Blazers.

Hockey in Oklahoma just shrieks irony. It's a paradox. Or, one would think. But it's true, one of the "warm weather" states, Oklahoma, had a professional hockey team and I was on it.

I do remember snow in the forecast there, and when it fell, the cozy, passive flatland expanse misshaped itself into a statewide emergency. We got about a ½ inch or so one time, a dusting, when the National Guard came marching in to restore order as panic spread throughout the region. As for us hockey guys from Canada, the flurries felt like home.

As uninterested as I was in the past to experience one abridged journey after the next as a professional hockey player, I will admit, Oklahoma City was a great place. I played with a bunch of young, single, exuberant guys down there like Teddy Irvine, Phil "Skippy" Krake, Jean-Paul Parise, and Wayne Cashman. "Cash" was the best teammate I ever had in my playing career. All he cared about was winning. And he was probably the best corner guy I had ever seen in hockey. Derek Sanderson came to Oklahoma City toward the end of the season.

We hung out at a place called The Jungle Pitt down there. It was owned by a guy named Jacko. He had a pet monkey that tagged along with him everywhere he went, including the bar. By the end of each day, Jacko was covered with whatever came out of that monkey's ass from dusk till dawn. It was foul! But a haven for some of the local fly colonies, no doubt.

Skippy and I especially enjoyed going there. The beer was only about 2 percent alcohol, so we could sit there and hang out longer than we would normally at another place…about 98 percent longer!

It was that first year in Oklahoma City when I met Harry Sinden.

Harry was a player/coach for the Blazers, and that year was skating in his last season as a professional. He retired as a player, but in the subsequent years he left an unambiguous mark on hockey as a great head coach and general manager for the Boston Bruins.

My first year in Oklahoma City, 1965–66, was a good one. I played in thirty games recording a 2.49 GAA, and the team won the Central Hockey League championship.

It was a painstaking road to the finals for me. I had dislocated my shoulder three times that year, but I kept playing. When it was time to have surgery, the doctors felt I didn't need it. The thought was, because I played through the pain, I may have actually strengthened it in the process. I never popped it again.

The summer came and went in uneventful fashion. When training camp approached for the 1966–67 campaign, I came in determined to make the Bruins and become a mainstay as one of the goalies on the "big club's" roster. I had nothing else to prove in the minors. I put up good numbers, and I knew I could play at the NHL level—and play well.

Little did the organization know that a new era would usher in Boston Bruins hockey, and the NHL, beginning that year. The new era was marked by the arrival of one Robert Gordon Orr. Bobby Orr was a rising star, and over time, his talent and capacity for the game simply commanded change.

It was in training camp, in London, Ontario, when we got our first glimpse of Orr. Whether it was a scrimmage or just a drill, Bobby had the puck the whole time it seemed, and did what he wanted with it. He had a good burst of speed and a wicked shot. I saw him let a blast go that whistled past a kid's ear; the winger in front of the net turned white. Suffice it to say, we knew this was a guy who was going to help the Bruins win a lot of games.

Orr was a gentleman, a polite kid. And he was young, just eighteen when he first arrived in Boston. I had him over for dinner once, and at the conclusion of the meal he said to my wife, "Thanks, Mrs. Cheevers." After he left I said to my wife, "Pretty soon, it's going to be, 'Mr. Orr.' You know that, right?"

I made the team that year. I played in 22 games and recorded a 3.33 GAA for the Bruins. But, again, I would be sent down to Oklahoma City. Murray Davison was now the head coach that year, taking over for Harry. He was a teammate of mine on the Blazers the year before. Frazier Gleason was the trainer.

Off the ice we hit a bar called The Roundtable. It was owned by a guy named Jay, a military guy who had already finished a tour in Vietnam in recon. Jay was an interesting guy. He took care of us well. The place had a few pool tables, so we played a lot when we were there.

Rudy "Pete" Panagabko was another teammate of mine, and like myself, fancied a game of pool from time to time. Pete and I played a couple of guys in pool one night for a few bucks, and had pretty good success. Panagabko would play safe, and I'd sink the balls in. The two foes kept leaving the bar, coming back, and bringing more money, so we did the only thing we could think of that seemed logical. We kept taking it. The next few days, however, guys were coming in donning their pinky rings, and shiny, overly garish pool cases looking for us to play a few games. That's when we called it quits. These guys could have been hustlers for all we knew.

But what stuck out in my mind that year wasn't the fool hearted pool players and their generous donations. It was the fact that I hadn't seen my daughter, Sherril, since she was born in March, just a couple of months prior. I didn't like it. So to avoid another significant lapse in time where I would be away from my family, I decided to make a move—or more appropriately stated, I wanted to stay put. I approached the Bruins and asked if I could sign a ten-year contract to stay in Oklahoma City for somewhere in the vicinity of $8,000–$9,000 annually. I wanted to stay there the rest of my career, and it made sense. The money would be doable, to live a good life in Oklahoma, and more importantly, I could raise my family there without any unmanageable interludes that would result in having little or no contact with my wife and kids.

But management didn't go for it. So, I continued forward into uncertainty.

The 1967–68 season proved to be anything but lackluster, and when we suited up against the Oilers of Tulsa, that truth never became so evident.

Tulsa was about one hundred miles from Oklahoma City, which, in a vast, rural state like Oklahoma, some would consider the organization's neighbors. Though the Oilers had just joined the league in 1964, truth be told, Tulsa and Oklahoma City were gripped in a heated rivalry. The fans had no idea what they were cheering for, though. They knew the clock stopped on the whistle. They knew it was a goal when the puck went in the net. And when a player was escorted by a referee and sat down by himself, away from his teammates in a little box for a few minutes, he probably did something bad. But beyond that, they were clueless as to the rules of hockey. What they could recognize quite easily was a good scuffle, and we had a groovy one with Tulsa.

During a game in Tulsa's arena, a fight broke out that carried into the stands. From there, after the game, tempers flared again. Only this time it was our trainer, Frazier Gleason, who would be the instigator. The chubby little trainer incited a brawl by taking a swing at a guy, and the next thing we knew it was mayhem. It was a tough night. We got into a lot of trouble. After the game, in the dressing room, the authorities were looking for Frazier, so we stuck him in a stick bag and loaded him on the bus. We forgot about him in there until about thirty minutes later into our trip home. The lack of oxygen in the fetal position nearly killed him. Another half hour and it might have been lights out for Frazier.

Dick Cherry, the brother of Don Cherry, was a defenseman on the team that year in Oklahoma City. Dick was a good hockey player who split a lot of his career between the Bruins and Flyers organizations. Off the ice, Dick was a bird watcher and a karate expert; a peculiar combination to say the least. Nonetheless, we roomed together from time to time on the road that season.

We had a home game one night in "OK" City. That afternoon, before the contest, the show The World of Golf had aired on television, but Dick, an avid watcher of the show, had missed it. I happened to catch it that day as I was relaxing before the game. After the contest we headed to Tulsa to take on the dreaded Oilers. We left on the bus late that evening and arrived in Tulsa around 2AM. The following day, as I was again resting before the game, the show The World of Golf was once again airing on television. It was a repeat from the day before. I couldn't help myself. I started putting wagers on each hole with Dick, betting on different shots each golfer was taking, knowing the outcome ahead of time. It was a goof. We had a good laugh over it. I never would have taken any money from him because he was a teammate, and more importantly, he could have crane-kicked my ass back to Oklahoma City if he wanted.

It was there, back in Oklahoma City, where something lay still. It was the most elegant, picturesque, saintly vision of a specimen; at least that's what Teddy Irvine thought of his '57 Pontiac. It was his pride and joy, the apple of his eye, his baby. The car was in pristine condition, and all but ready to be featured in a showroom, if Teddy so desired. Aesthetically speaking, the vehicle commanded respect; and so did Teddy, the day he unthinkingly let me drive it.

It was harmless. I was driving without a shred of apprehension—until the car began to feel a little warm…then the smoke…then the panic. The car was overheating! I pulled over hurriedly and got out. There was a bonfire under the hood, big enough to send smoke signals to Jersey. So I stepped back, farther and farther away, and took cover when the car exploded, shaking the foundation which it rested on.

Teddy was devastated when I delivered the news, because for all intents and purposes, a member of his extended family was now gone. I apologized sincerely. He had tears in his eyes. I had tears in my eyes. The spectacle had an eerie resemblance to when my color-by-number painting took a dirt nap at the hands of someone else. Only this time, it was no one's fault. The car had just had enough…I think.

Teddy got over it after some time. He actually lived next door to me in an apartment along with Joe Watson, a defenseman from Smithers, BC.

Watson's dad came up to visit one time and joined us on a little road trip. As it turned out, we would forego the road and take by air. We boarded a small DCA plane piloted by Rocky Robertson, who was the brother of Dale Robertson, the famed Hollywood actor, well known for his role as Jim Hardie from the hit TV series, Tales of Wells Fargo. Rocky was one of the most confident pilots I had ever seen. He was a bootlegger back in the day. Rocky had a sixth sense that could detect trouble if it were lurking nearby, and because of this keen awareness, the man could land a plane in a school yard if he had to.

Joe's dad was a big guy, a heavy guy. And the fact that we had an "ace" manning the controls did little to ease his anxiety about flying. Unfortunately, Joe's dad was feeling anxious, so much so that we had to hurdle over him to get around on the plane because he decided to nap in the aisle. The trip, however, ended without incident.

Bill Goldsworthy, God rest his soul, was another dynamic teammate of mine in Oklahoma City, and quite a character. We were both hurt at the same time that year, so we spent a lot of time together.

When Bill finally got off the shelf, he was to play in one game to get ready for the playoffs. It was the last game of the season, and to the organization, that meant award ceremony time. Before the game, a mat was laid out on the ice in preparation before the honors for the year were to be given out. I didn't play that game, so I was watching comfortably from the stands. Before the formal procedure Bill was warming up, skating around, and daringly jumping the mat repeatedly. Regrettably, he hit the carpet on a pass, sending "Goldsy" through the trophy stand and devastating the area, scattering the awards all over the place. For poor Bill, whatever could have gone wrong in that sequence did. However, after the tumble the awards were given out…after some were pieced back together.

That year, in Oklahoma City, I would finish the season playing in just 26 games. However, it would be en route to another championship season.

That summer the Blazers ran a hockey school in Oklahoma City for the locals. It was Frazier Gleason's brain child. I remember vividly that it was hot like Hades one day, as fifty kids showed up eager to learn the game brought down from the frigid temperatures of the great white north. But the kids' enthusiasm didn't hide the fact that what they failed to realize was that this game ain't that easy.

Most of the kids arrived with the idea that if they couldn't skate, they were meant to play goalie. So out of fifty kids, thirty of them wanted to be goaltenders. With only four sets of pads available, we had to change some of their minds. I took a couple of lads, put the pads on them, and sent them out on the ice, in net. A moment later, I whistled a few slap shots by their ears. Their ignorance was replaced with fear and reality. The camp ended up with four goaltenders.

A few days into the camp a kid came in crying, telling us someone stole his hockey pants. We looked intently on finding the pants, but had no luck, until I noticed a little black kid skating around with them. Prior to that day, this kid never had hockey pants, so I knew he was the culprit. I asked him if they were his, and he confessed they weren't. So I let him know he couldn't just take someone's gear and put it on; it didn't work like that. But the poor kid really had no idea. There was no malicious intent on his part. So the kid returned the pants and went out on the ice with just a long sweater reminiscent of a lady's cocktail dress. During the flow of a scrimmage game, the kid lost his balance, hit the ice, and in doing so, his shirt came up, revealing a lot more than we bargained. He was bare ass. Maybe taking someone's underwear would have been a better choice after all.

In the latter end of the summer of 1967, I was twenty-six years old. My hope that my career would come full circle was beginning to wither. But it was in that same year that the NHL touted the idea of expanding from its "Original Six," to a twelve-team league. They had to. The networks were strongly considering televising games from the Western Hockey League instead, unless the additions of more clubs were made.

The idea of expansion had become a reality, and just ahead would come the expansion draft. Each existing team was only allowed to protect one goaltender. The Bruins had a good core group of goaltenders at the time, including Bernie Parent, Ed Johnston, Dougie Favell, and, of course, me. Never did I suspect I'd be wearing a Bruins' uniform that season, but I did. As astonishing as it was to me, the organization decided to retain me.

That summer I trained pretty hard, determined on proving the organization did right in keeping me. I was through playing lacrosse by this time, but I still ran a lot. I wanted to shed a few pounds as well. I went as far as driving around in my car with the heat blasting, with a dry-cleaning bag draped over my body so I could sweat off the pounds just to drop some weight.

I joined the St. Catharines Golf Club that off season, as did Freddy Stanfield, who was acquired via trade from the Chicago Blackhawks, along with Phil Esposito and Ken Hodge, for Pit Martin, Jack Norris, and Gille Marotte. The trade was considered over time to be one of the more lopsided transactions in hockey history. Everyone knew Phil was a talent, a playmaker, and the centerpiece of the trade. But no one knew Hodge and Stanfield would develop into stars in their own right. The trade garnered so much attention, everyone wanted to take credit for it, including my dear friend, Zibby, the head of the Bull-Gang, the crew who took care of the Boston Garden ice.

Freddy actually lived just one block away from me, and was a member of the St. Catharines Teepees. We played golf everyday with Dougie Favell, and Dougie Robinson, who were both St. Catharines natives. Robinson was a member of the Rangers organization at the time. It was that summer when I really developed a love for golf.

Favell was the other goaltender for that Oklahoma City team. We hung out together and shared our thoughts on goaltending a lot. Dougie was a great athlete and went on to have a pretty good career in the NHL. Even today, we play a lot of golf together whenever I come home to St. Catharines. He remains a very good friend of mine.

Now the 1967–68 season was upon us. This team, the Bruins, was a talented bunch, and by season's end it showed, at least in the stat sheet. Orr was doing his thing at the blue line, scoring 11 goals and assisting on 20 more. "Espo" led the team in goals with 35. Johnny Bucyk, John McKenzie, and Ken Hodge had outstanding offensive years. I played in 47 games, recording a 2.83 GAA, sharing the goaltending duties with Eddie Johnston.

Life was good as a Bruin, but for the life of me, I still could not get my mother to a game to watch me play, even if I traveled to Toronto to take on the Maple Leafs!

It was a ritual, a ceremonial happening that when we played in Toronto, my friends and family would come to the game, and the same went for any other guy who grew up in that area. His family would come, too.

I don't know how it happened, maybe the stars were aligned that day, but I finally managed to sway her to come to a game, even though I already knew I wasn't starting. Go figure. I invited my mom and her girlfriend. They came the night before the game and stayed overnight at The Royal York. We had a beautiful dinner that night, and the following day I took them both out to lunch. Eddie Johnston started that game, and I remember we won handily by a 5–1 score. After the game I asked mom if she enjoyed herself, and she said, "I was a nervous wreck."

"Why?"

"When you sit on the bench," she said. "And you had your hands hanging over the boards, I was so afraid you would get hit with the puck."

But despite my mom finally giving in to making the trek to see her son at work, and the observable surge in everyone's play, in '69 we finished 3rd in the East Division behind the 2nd place New York Rangers, and the division champion Montreal Canadiens. We did, however, smugly lead the league in penalty minutes (PIM) with 1,043.

The playoffs began and ended in a blink of an eye. We opened against the Montreal Canadiens, and about a week later I was on the links trying to improve my short game. We got swept 4–0. But the Canadiens were stout. They won in 5 games over the Blackhawks in round 2, then swept the St. Louis Blues to win the Stanley Cup.

As the off season began to diminish, my desire to make more money for the upcoming season began to surface. I made $11,000 the previous year, but wanted a pay increase that would get me to $15,000. This would be the first year I'd use an agent to handle my negotiations, and his name was Alan Eagleson.

Eagleson was a renowned hockey agent around the league, with a future that would eventually include disbarment as a Canada attorney and a felony conviction. He would become a politician, a promoter, and the Executive Director of the Player's Association, a position he held for twenty-five years.

Alan was Orr's agent. I met him through Bobby one day at the Radio and Artists Club in Toronto where we had our pre-game meals. I knew who he was, but I never formally met him. After the pleasantries were exchanged, I asked him if he would represent me. He agreed, and then swiftly sent me a bill for $250. I should have known, then, that this was a little peculiar.

I told Alan I wanted to make $15,000 for the 1968–69 season. His advice to me was to hold out. Guys today hold out for millions. I held out for $4,000. But that was then. That was the climate in professional sports in the 60s. Anyway, I told Alan in no uncertain terms that I had plenty of fun in training camp the year before, and I wasn't missing it. He said, "You're not going to play any games." I agreed.

I kept on Alan, asking how the negotiations were going. He led on, the more we hold out, the better the outcome will be.

Finally, the Bruins had one game pre-season contest left. I told Alan I was playing. I had to get one game in before the season started. He was adamant, telling me I'd lose my leverage if I played. I didn't care what anyone said, I was playing in that game. He advised against it. I played.

Eagleson called me the next day and said, "I got you $13,000. That's the middle point between $11,000 and $15,000." After I verified his math with a calculator, I told him to sign it. I wanted to be done with it. So he signed it, and two weeks later I got a bill for $2,000 from Alan. Simple arithmetic told me my paycheck would look eerily similar to the year before.

What a treasure Eagleson turned out to be. That was the end of him as my agent.

In the 1968–69 campaign the team really began to gel. Orr had established himself as the best player in the game, and Espo had his best year to date offensively, recording 49 goals and 77 assists, consequently winning the Hart Trophy for being the league's most valuable player. I played in 52 games, finishing with a 2.80 GAA. Led by Harry Sinden behind the bench, we finished this time in 2nd place with 100 points, just 3 points behind last year's Stanley Cup champions, the Montreal Canadiens.

We breezed through the 1st round, sweeping the Toronto Maple Leafs in 4 games, but not without paying a price. The series would be stained by a violent hit. The victim was Bobby Orr, and the perpetrator was a rookie named Pat Quinn.

That particular year I roomed with Orr for a period of time, and, in fact, we were mates the night Pat Quinn laid a vicious body check on Bobby that rendered him unconscious. It was an ugly night, as the hit instigated a brawl between the Maple Leafs and the Bruins. Fans were throwing everything under the sun directed at Quinn. He was lucky he made it out of there alive. When the smoke cleared, Bobby left the ice with a concussion. That night, I remember waking him up periodically to make sure he was still 'with it.' He was okay after all, and well enough to play the following day.

In those days a concussion was treated with a couple of aspirin and a 'call me in the morning.' The National Hockey League, as well as a number of other professional sports organizations, has come a long way in that regard.

After we disposed of Toronto, it was on to face the dreaded Canadiens. They were a perennial power, and they had seemed to lose little of their might, if any, as last year's Cup-winning team.

We were a lucky bounce or two away from winning the East Division, and we knew we had the stuff to be champions. So going in we felt confident.

It was hard fought, but we came up on the losing end of a 4-2 series.

It was a bitter end to a season filled with excitement, honors, and the realization that we had a great chance to win a Stanley Cup, if we could only get past the Montreal Canadiens.

The off season, to a degree, took on a similar feel for me, in that I still had contract issues and no agent in my corner to handle the negotiations.

During the 1960s, a prominent Boston attorney had garnered a lot of attention representing some of the more well known athletes in the area. His name was Bob Woolf. I sought him out and hired him. Bob turned out to be a good guy, an honorable guy. I never had a problem with him as a person or an agent.

I was looking for something in the neighborhood of $18,000–$20,000 a year, which was about the norm at the time for an established net minder with some success under his belt.

Bob set up an appointment with then General Manager Milt Schmidt to begin negotiations. I was unaware that Bob Woolf was also representing Eddie Johnston, the Bruins' other goalie. So Bob told Milt he was looking for $18,000–$20,000 for Eddie as well. When Milt counter offered my contract he used Eddie Johnston as leverage, implying the team had another quality goaltender already. When he counter offered Eddie's, he used me as leverage, implying the same thing. It was a fleeting moment of irony, and a bit on the uncomfortable side, but in the end a deal got made. I settled for $17,000 for one year.

Contract wise, the pressure was off for at least another year. And with the group of guys coming back for another go-around, expectations were beginning to run high, and rightly so. We felt we were good enough to win a Stanley Cup, and anything less would be a disappointment. This is the year we would turn the corner.

1969–1972

The 1969–70 season began with high hopes, but before we got our bearings, we had to make it out of the pre season intact.

In an exhibition game in Ottawa, against the St. Louis Blues, one of our defensemen, Teddy Green, was engaged in a swinging stick match with Blues' forward, Wayne Maki. Green was struck in the head badly, and as a result, suffered a severe injury and nearly lost his life.

Maki was just a scared, young kid. When the sticks went up, he didn't know what to do, so he started swinging. It was an awful scene. Consequently, Teddy Green missed the entire 1969–70 season.

When something like that happens it's difficult to pick up the pieces right away. We were deflated. It was demoralizing to the team, and especially to Teddy. He was coming off a very good year for the Bruins in '69 when he was voted on to the all-star team. He was a big loss to the team, a hollow fact considering he nearly lost his life that day.

So the 1969–70 season had an auspicious beginning, but we recovered, and developed great team chemistry among the players. We had a rule: Whenever we decided to go out for a few pops, everyone had to go for at least one beer, whether at home or on the road. At home, it was more difficult because guys lived in different areas of the suburbs, but on the road it was easier to get people together. Any absences were met with a kangaroo court fine. Each time it was either a way to let out some frustrations after a tough loss, or to relish a victory. Other times we'd throw a team party where the wives would mingle as well. Everyone knew everyone.

By season's end we were a talented, hard working and cohesive unit, and it showed. Bobby had a breakout year offensively, nearly doubling his point total from last season, recording 33 goals and 87 assists. Phil's totals dropped off a bit, perhaps due to the team's balanced attack. He was still sensational. I stayed on course, finishing with a 2.72 GAA.

But to say we cruised to the top of the East Division standings would be a lie. We tied Chicago for first with 99 points, and lost the tie-breaker. And though the Canadiens finished 7 points behind us, they missed the playoff entirely. In the West, it was the St. Louis Blues defending their division title and finishing in 1st place for the 2nd year in a row.

Standings, points, and other ancillary statistics didn't matter to us. We were poised to win a championship that year.

In the 1st round of the playoffs we faced the New York Rangers. We took the first two games at home in convincing fashion, which frustrated both the Rangers and their fans. They were shouting obscenities and tossing foreign objects at all of us as game 1 was underway. It was a nightmarish situation. The game and series showcased brawls from one end of the ice to the other. The fan abuse climaxed when they set fire to the Madison Square Garden mezzanine. Thankfully, we got out of New York alive, and with a 4–2 series win.

No one said the playoffs would be easy, but in round 2 we clicked in all phases and swept the Blackhawks in 4.

It was on to the finals.

The Blues had three outstanding goaltenders, Ernie Wakely, Jacques Plante, and Glenn Hall. They split playing time pretty evenly that year, and all three were among the league leaders in GAA that season. In fact, Wakely led overall with a 2.11 GAA.

Despite the Blues fielding the great goaltending tandem, and the fact that St. Louis was making their third straight Stanley Cup finals appearance, we were heavily favored to win the series.

And as fate would have it, in game 1 of the series, Phil Esposito would redirect a slap shot from Freddy Stanfield, splitting Plante's mask at his forehead, knocking him out cold. The injury sidelined Plante for the rest of the series. But it was Glenn Hall, and not Wakely, who would step in and play the rest of the way. Hall had given way to Wakely as a starting goaltender during the regular season. But when it counted, in the finals, the Blues went with the seasoned veteran in Hall.

The injury to Plante was unfortunate, and had been deemed a devastating blow to the Blues, but to my eye, it made no difference as to the outcome of the series. It didn't matter who was in net, we were too strong.

We took the first three games convincingly behind the strong play of Phil Esposito who had led the post-season play with 27 points. In game 4 we jumped out to a 3–1 lead, and by my own omission, we should have won that game in regulation. I had a tendency to let my guard down when we were ahead, and in a finals game, I couldn't have picked a worse time to drop the armor. I had felt I let in a couple of easy goals, and in doing so, the Blues tied the game, thus sending the contest into overtime, and setting up one of the most celebrated goals in hockey history.

Noel Picard, a Montreal native and defenseman for the Blues, was on the ice when it happened. He was a pleasant guy to be around, and incongruously, had a career that ran parallel to mine, to a degree. He bounced around for several years in the minors before he finally found a home with the Blues in 1967. It was so hot playing in the Boston Garden back then (and of course, in that series) that Picard became almost delirious. He was so disoriented that, after a shift, he sat on our bench by accident. None of the guys told him, they let him sit there in his trance-like state.

Little did we know then that the often jovial Noel Picard would someday be synonymous with the most famous act of frustration at the moment of defeat in a Stanley Cup series: He tripped Bobby Orr as he scored the winning goal in overtime of game 4. But make no mistake about it: It was a blatant act of refusing to accept the fact that the Blues would be swept in the finals for the 3rd consecutive year.

And thanks to my shabby play, letting two slip past me late in that game, the world may never have known who Bobby Orr was…or maybe they would have.

But over the course of history, the words shouted from the broadcast booth by the late Don Earle, "Sanderson to Orr!" has resonated among hockey fans all over the world. When it happened I got so excited I threw my stick in the air, but when it landed it caught the top of the glass behind the net and just hovered for a few moments. Guys were yelling to get the stick down, and when it finally fell, it came down on the ice side. So I got to the pile-up a little later than the other guys, but it mattered little, as the fun was just beginning.

It was exciting to say the least. For me and the guys, it was our first championship together after a couple of disappointing finales the two years prior. For the organization, it was a sweet birth into the expansion era, considering the team hadn't won a Stanley Cup since the 1940–41 season when guys like Bobby Bauer, Eddie Wiseman, and Bill Cowley were lighting the lamp for the Bruins.

After the game, in the locker room, it was mayhem. Guys were bathing in champagne as the corks were popping irregularly from every direction. From wall to wall, the place was teeming with reporters, photographers, and close family and friends of the players.

Don Earle called the Bruins' games on television for WSBK-TV from 1967–1971. He gripped the mic that night, weaved his way through the pandemonium, and began interviewing all the guys. It seemed that each guy put in plain words that it was the greatest day of their lives.

It was so hectic that Eddie Johnston, Patty Considine, and I snuck into the stick room where we had our own case of beer waiting. Patty ran the penalty box and helped out a lot around the dressing room. He was a dear friend of ours. We hung out for a few, and when we finished up I was walked back to the main room. On my journey, there was my father, holding court in a press conference, with reporters sticking microphones in his face, hanging on every word he was saying. My dad was famous for stepping up to the mic, though. He was good at it; he could rap with the media like it was nobody's business.

A lot of the parents were there celebrating with their sons in the locker room, including Doug Orr, Bobby's dad. They both interviewed with Don Earle.

It was just a great time, a tremendous atmosphere. To this day I enjoy looking at the pictures and reminiscing about that night.

After we left the Garden that night, we went to George Page's Colonial with all the parents and friends of the team. Sadly, my dad, who had a history of heart problems, had a mild heart attack that night, and was rushed to the Lynn Hospital where he'd spend ten days recuperating, if you will. He was a celebrity in a gurney. The nurses took to his charm like a pack of school girls at an Elvis Presley meet and greet. My dad had a way; his presence was palpable. Thankfully, he made a full recovery.

The victory parade running through the streets of Boston was one of the more vigorous celebrations I had ever been involved in. I met more people in that one day that I became friends with than during the previous ten years. Every place we hit after we got off the motorcade wanted to buy us a beer. The fans really embraced us as heroes that day. I'll never forget it. It was a great celebration. During that time in Boston, the Celtics were perennial champions in the NBA; but to my recollection, the way the people of Boston responded to the C's winning an NBA title was nothing compared to what we experienced. A closer comparison to our celebration would be the New England Patriots in 2001 when they beat the Rams in the Super Bowl. After seeing how the city responded then, it was reminiscent of our 1970 experience.

The following night a bunch of us ended up meeting at the 99 Restaurant near the Garden. Of course, today, the 99 Restaurant has prospered since into a major restaurant chain located primarily in the northeast; in 1970 it was just finding its bearings. We'd become friendly with the bartender up there, Tommy Marr. Tommy was actually a world-class comedian, so there was some entertainment value there as well.

Often times, a lot of us would have lunch there, and because we were the Bruins, a simple meal could turn into a Broadway show. And because of the antics we brought, I'd say scores of people on their lunch break probably never made it back to work on a day we showed up.

On the first night following the festivities, after the motorcade parade in the city, another celebration was at hand, and the location was the 99. Though the magnitude was significantly less, the fun never seemed to lack any potency.

It was a good night, and one that brought a more precarious ambiance, at least by today's standards. We used to hang out on the third floor of the restaurant, and while we were well into celebration "dos," one of our players took a police motorcycle that was parked in front of the restaurant, wheeled it into the elevator, and pressed floor #3. When the doors opened he carted the bike in and set it in the middle of the bar. But it was no harm done. The cop made his way up to the bar and cared little of his bike being transported to the bar under his nose. Everyone had fun that night.

Winning the Cup meant a lot to me personally. Like most other athletes playing a sport, professional or otherwise, I wanted to win a championship. And as a professional hockey player, the coveted prize was the Stanley Cup, so when it finally happened it served as a significant accomplishment in my career. It had been ten years in the making, and keeping that in mind throughout my career, I felt bad for a lot of guys who never had the opportunity to experience the joy of winning like I did. I had always believed had I not been on a winning team as a professional hockey player, my career would have been marked by a considerable void. But I was lucky enough to get to Boston, which allowed me to play with some great players.

On a cheerful note, Teddy Green was coming along nicely, and it was good to see his name engraved on the Cup.

Of course, like any major sports championship series, things tend to get overlooked. And I mean that in a most mocking fashion. In a finals game that year I unofficially assisted on 2 goals in the same period, but never got credit for them. The puck came back to our end; I left it for Bobby, he went through the Blues' defense like they were standing still, and scored. On the 2nd goal, I left it for Bobby, he went through the Blues' defense again, just as easy, and then passed it to Johnny Bucyk for the score. No one cared if a goalie got an assist back then, and I'd never be fickle enough to bring it up in an earnest fashion. It gave me a chuckle more than anything, and it does to this day.

So now the team, the organization, and its fans were brought together by a victory they hadn't experienced in quite some time. After the 1941 Stanley Cup season, the Bruins were unable to sustain that level of excellence, and it was likely due to the fact they lost a lot of their top talent to the War. For us, we knew if the team's roster remained intact, we'd be poised to win another Cup. But as soon as the champagne dried, and the streets were devoid of confetti, the news came down: The organization would be looking to replace our head coach, Harry Sinden.

After contract negotiations stalled with Bruins' management, Harry decided to step down as head coach to take a job in Rochester, New York, with a prefab construction company called Stirling Homex Corporation. Following Sinden's departure, the Bruins named Tom Johnson as their new head coach.

On the flip side, Teddy Green had made a full recovery, and was once again guarding the blue line for us on defense.

I hit the negotiation table once again, this time signing a one-year deal for $35,000.

The 1970–71 season seemed like a party all year. We were still celebrating winning the Cup a year ago, if not in the open, to ourselves.

I roomed with Mike "Shaky" Walton for a period of time that season. Shaky wasn't part of the championship team, but he was quite a character, and one of Bobby's good buddies. They ran a summer camp together back in Ontario.

Not a care in the world we had that year. We even locked up in a meaningless game, which lacked the intensity we were accustomed to seeing between us rivals. It was rare, but it did happen. But the contest had no bearing on the playoffs; where we would be seeded or anyone else.

During a play in our end, the puck came off the back boards. John Ferguson, an enforcer who played wing for the Canadiens, had his head down in front of the net. I wanted to give him a good shot, a clean shot to the body. But before my chance presented itself, he calls out to me. "Cheesie!" I stopped and stood up. "Hoist the Flag broke his leg this morning!"

"What?" I asked.

"Hoist the Flag" was a thoroughbred horse, a champion, and heavily favored to win the Kentucky Derby that year. Being a horse owner, it was of great interest to me. So much so, I lost connection with what I was doing for that brief second. And instead of me laying out Fergy, Fergy laid me out, and then he started laughing.

That was one of the few times a Boston-Montreal bout wasn't too serious.

For someone on the outside looking in, seemingly, we had a very good year. Personally, I won 27 games and finished with a 2.73 GAA. Statistically speaking, everyone did their part in the regular season, including our rookie coach, Tom Johnson.

Tom was a good boss. He coached us the way we wanted to be coached. In fact, when the regular season concluded, we finished with 121 points, 22 more than the Stanley Cup champion team the year before. But despite finishing in first place atop the East once again, we moseyed into the playoffs, rather lethargic, and paid the price.

We faced off against the Montreal Canadiens in one of the most intense series we'd played to date. In the end we succumbed to them in 7 games.

As a team we just didn't work, so we weren't prepared. We took things for granted, and thought we'd win another Cup without showing up, but that wasn't the case. The loss was painful, and a lesson learned. We were still celebrating winning the Cup the year before when the series began.

And though there was a slight change in coaching philosophy from Sinden to Johnson, this loss was on the players. We didn't bring it like we knew we could. We simply lacked the desire we had grasped so tightly the year before. All we could do was focus on the season ahead.

I don't have much to say about '71. I never really dwelled on losses such as this one, or stayed up late at night wondering what went wrong, or what could I have done better to help the team. In anomalous fashion, I slept like a baby when we lost. I wanted to put it out of my mind as fast as I could, and that was the most efficient way. When we won, I couldn't sleep at night. I reveled in the key points of the game that brought us to victory. After game 7, I got a good eight hours in.

Now we would be tested, to see how we would bounce back from a disappointing finale that year. Losing the way we did was the mark of a team that wasn't focused. But overcoming adversity is the mark of a champion. Only time would tell which path our team would follow.

From the outset of the 1971–72 season it was obvious we came to play. We were confident as always, but this time we dug in, focused, and set a course to win another Stanley Cup.

Bobby and Phil led the leagues in scoring, and I had myself a nice 32-game unbeaten streak which lasted until the second to last game of the season. I remember it vividly. In what would have been game 33 in the streak, neither Orr nor Esposito dressed for that contest. As a result, it was 4–0, Toronto, at the 10-minute mark. You figure it out. To my eye, their absence served as a strong indicator as to how important those guys were to the team. Truth be told, I struggled early on until I finally hit my stride, which was when the streak began.

Overall, we made few mistakes that year, if any. And at times it seemed like we could score at will. We were a tough team, too, with some of the most physical players in the league like Derek Sanderson, Eddie Westfall, and Donny Marcotte laying hits all over the ice. The Bruins in the 70s were a great forechecking team as well, but it's never talked about. It was something we hung our hat on, along with all the scoring records we piled up.

We were a team on a mission, and by season's end, we took the division once again, outlasting the New York Rangers by 10 points.

When the regular season came to a close, Tom Johnson had informed me that I'd be alternating starts with Eddie Johnston in the post season, which was fine. Eddie had a terrific regular season, so it was a good move.

In round 1 of the playoffs, we faced off against the Toronto Maple Leafs. The Leafs barely qualified for the post season, finishing just 2 games above .500. We pounced on them as soon as the puck dropped in game 1, beating them 5–0. They nipped us in overtime in game 2 by a score of 4–3, before we ran off 3 straight victories to take the series 4–1.

In round 2 we'd take on our old foes from St. Louis. The Blues had just come off a tough 7-game series with the Minnesota North Stars, so they were ripe for the picking.

This was never a series. In games 1 and 2, we outscored the Blues by a 16–3 margin, en route to disjointing St. Louis in 4 games.

Waiting for us in the finals were the New York Rangers. Though the Rangers played in a few nail biters in their series with the Blackhawks, they sent Chicago home in 4 games.

So both teams were coming off sweeps, and both were well rested.

We took the first 2 games in Boston, winning both contests by 1 goal. I started game 3, but lost. We had a 2–1 series advantage when Eddie got the call for game 4 and played great. We won 3–2.

With a 3–1 lead in the series we started to feel good. We knew we were on the verge of winning our 2nd Cup in three years. I was slated to start game 5, but with the team on the brink of ending the series, I went to Tom Johnson and made a pitch. I told him if he wanted to start Eddie, it was quite alright with me. "Don't ever worry about me," I said. Very smug, I went on, "If something happens, throw me in, in game 6."

Eddie was having a fantastic post season. Moreover, I was in net when we beat St. Louis in '70, so it was Eddie's chance to relish a victory when the clock ran out. He deserved this. Tom had no problem with it, so he started Eddie.

But it would turn out to be New York's day. The Rangers came out, with their backs against the wall, and played great. Eddie played well, but it wasn't enough. In the end they squeaked by, beating us 3–2.

Game 6 would move to Madison Square Garden, one of the more hostile places to play. It was the sight of the famous frustration-induced meltdown by the fans from a couple of years ago.

After the game 5 loss we had our heads down. Perhaps we came into the game a little too confident. We really thought we were going to win. When we didn't, it stung.

The following day was an off day, but I went out and practiced, which was rare for me when given the opportunity to rest. But my sentiments ran parallel with the rest of the team, in that I wanted to end this thing. We didn't want to go to a game 7.

I got the start in game 6.

It wasn't a very physical game, not by our standards, but it did shape a fight between Derek Sanderson and Rod Gilbert in that deciding game. The puck was tied up along the boards, and before they could dig it out, Derek was exchanging shots with Gilbert before the refs got between them. Poor Rod Gilbert never fought anyone. He certainly picked the wrong guy to tangle with that day. He lost.

It was a raucous crowd at the Garden that night, as always, but it didn't matter. We came out focused and ran them over, beating the Rangers 3–0 and winning the Stanley Cup once again.

Bobby had an outstanding game, scoring a couple of goals, and he was awarded the Conn Smythe Trophy as the post season's most valuable player. The shutout was to be regarded with wariness. There must have been 10 shots that went behind me that either hit a post or got deflected by a glove or a stick. Whatever the case, we were champions again.

Winning the Cup in 1970 was exceptional in its own right. It had been nearly three decades since the Bruins had won anything, and as a result, the popularity of some of the players like Orr, Esposito, Sanderson, and some of the other guys reached new heights. In '70 we beat an expansion team, the St. Louis Blues. But in '72, it was special. The Rangers were an Original Six team. This was sweet.

The '72 Bruins came together after a disappointing loss in the play-offs the year before, only to come back with a vengeance and beat a great hockey team in the Rangers. It was a team that grew up, a team that had become professionals.

Would the run continue?

Factors had developed internally and around the league that would change the landscape of hockey indefinitely; factors that would once again land me at the negotiating table, along with many others in hockey.

WORLD HOCKEY LEAGUE (WHA) PART I

By the early 1970s, the World Hockey League (WHA) had made significant headway in challenging the NHL's brass for custody of its own players. A newly created association exploited enough loopholes in players' contracts to allow them the wiggle room to move from one league to another. When all was said and done, a significant number of NHL players moved to the WHA, thus turning a relationship little to be regarded, into an acrimonious one. Nonetheless, a league was born; and it was one to be taken seriously.

While the battle off the ice had escalated, on the ice, we became world champions for the 2nd time in three years. But as much as I wanted to relish the victory, I had some business to tend to.

My contract would expire with the final game of the series. On the night before game 6 of the finals, Charlie Mulcahy, the club's legal counsel and Vice President, approached me while I was waiting at the airport in Boston. In not so many words, I told him to take a hike. His timing was less than accommodating, especially considering I was about to start in what many of us thought to be the deciding game in the Stanley Cup finals. I thought Charlie's actions weren't very proper, or professional. And I was right; we won game 6.

It wasn't until sometime toward the middle to the end of the summer—when I sat down with Charlie to negotiate a contract. I didn't have to dig deep to find the bargaining power needed to sign a deal with reasonable terms. I had just won my 2nd Stanley Cup, I lost just five games all year, and showed no signs of slowing down. But Charlie and the Bruins seemed to have felt differently.

I made $50,000 for the 71–72 season. Charlie offered me a $5k raise. I was taken aback. I got up and walked out.

I was shocked and very disappointed by the event, but I walked away with the understanding that it was a first offer, and there would be another on its way soon after.

A short time after the sit down with Charlie, my wife and I decided to take a weekend trip up to Montreal.

Though the excursion was meant to be one of a reposing nature, it was met with high flying action and suspense, when, while seated in a movie theater watching the Godfather I, just next door, a bank was being robbed. The assailant left the bank on foot, fleeing from the cops, and scampered through the theater right in front of our eyes! It was bonus footage we couldn't pay for and perhaps the inspiration for 3-D movies, because it never got any more real than that.

In the meantime, my friend, Larry Gordon, had moved to Boston the same time I had years ago. He and I went way back when we lived together in Rochester. Larry worked for Kimberly-Clark, but was the first to have merchandise that featured the Bruins and its players. He handled many of my affairs such as making public appearances at charity events or dinners, for a few extra bucks.

While still vacationing in Montreal, Larry gave me an unexpected call to inform me of two things: The New England Whalers of the WHA waived their right to acquire any Bruins out of respect for the Bruins. The second thing was, my rights had been traded to the Cleveland Crusaders and they would like to meet with me.

I was still less than moved over the Bruins' low-ball offer, but despite my fleeting disappointment with Boston, I was going to give them another chance. I told Larry I'd get back to him.

The Bruins came back and added another year to the deal, offering two years at $110,000.

Negotiations were tough back then, and if I approached them with anything less than ferocity, I'd be taken. "Here's my deal," I said. "I want $300k over 3 years. I don't care how you give it to me, as long as at the end of my contract, I'll be $300k richer."

And that's how I left it with Charlie. He was a shrewd businessman, but that was his job: to get me for as little as possible, and he always went about it that way.

I got back to Larry, and though I still wasn't taking Cleveland's interest in me seriously, I told Larry to make arrangements for some first-class tickets to Cleveland. We were going to go have some fun.

On the plane, over a couple of Bloody Marys, I told Larry he'll have to do the negotiating for me, as I never considered myself a wheeler and dealer at the table anyway.

"But know this," I said to Larry. "If I'm going to make his move, this is going to be a blockbuster deal. I want a million dollars over 4 years." Larry agreed.

We arrived safely at Cleveland Hopkins International Airport, eager to see what the newly born franchise had to offer. We were picked up at the gate by a man named Nick Mileti. This guy owned the Cleveland

Indians, Cleveland Cavaliers, Cleveland Barons of the AHL, a Cleveland AM radio station called "3WE," and, later, the Coliseum at Richfield. That's a lot. But he found the time to personally greet us with our bags in hand. It was a good indication.

Nick took us for lunch at the Cleveland Club. If I came away with anything during the first five minutes of our encounter, it was that Nick Mileti was one of the best guys I had ever met. He was a terrific gentleman and very down-to-earth. He never spoke over us, and made us feel at home.

So, four bloody marys later, after lunch, it was Larry's time. He was the negotiator. He was going to step up and wheel and deal over this gleaming white, seamless linen hanging by our belts. So Nick opened the discussion when he leaned over to me and asked, "What's the tariff price we have to meet to get you?"

Before Larry could pry his lips from his water glass, I blurted out, "A million dollars over four years."

Nick came back. "You got a deal!"

"What? Hold on," I said to Nick.

I told Nick I was kidding, but we're in the same ballpark. So I went on, forthright as can be. I told Nick at the present time I didn't want to come to Cleveland, I wanted to stay in Boston and play for the Bruins. I play with the best players in the world and we're going to win more championships. However, the money we just chucked around would be enough to influence a move to Cleveland for my family and I, assuming the contract would be guaranteed. Nick assured it was. "You and Larry go talk," he said. "We'll meet for dinner somewhere in downtown Cleveland."

That was that. Lunch and the preliminaries to our negotiation had concluded. Larry and I continued with the topic over a few drinks. I asked him point blank, "Is he serious?"

"Yeah, he is," Larry said.

Later that evening we met Nick for dinner. "I spoke to my people, and we want you," Nick said. "But we want you for 7 years. We'll give you something near $1.5 million."

That was a lot of money, not only for a professional hockey player, but for any pro athlete, anywhere in the world, in those days. However, we weren't done.

"Well, that's all fine and dandy," I said. "But I still want to play for the Bruins. So I'm going to give them one more chance to give me $100K a year for 3 years." I said, "It's stupid, but that's the way I am."

"I understand," Nick said.

We hopped on a plane and headed back to Boston, landing once again at the negotiating table. It didn't take long for me to realize, I was a long way from Cleveland. The Bruins came up to $60K a year. That wasn't going to work.

In the meantime, I had flown to Cleveland once again to iron out some of the more ancillary details of the contract if I was going to sign. The details were clauses I was putting in the deal, such as money for a home, a car, things like that. As this was taking place, whispers began to spread that I was working with the Crusaders on a deal to acquire me long term. As a result, a story was leaked to the papers. I had no comment, but it was enough to get the attention of the Bruins. So they came calling.

Tom Johnson, who was still the head coach of the Bruins, called me and said he'd love to meet me to discuss my future. I told him it was no problem, and that he knew where to find me, which was at Rockingham Park. We set up a meeting and met up on the roof of the race track.

From my camp, mums the word. I wasn't supposed to talk to anyone about my correspondence with Cleveland.

So Tom and I sat down to discuss my future. He began by saying the

Boston Bruins are offering me the same deal that Cleveland has offered me. I said, "Okay, Tom, they offered me $1.75 million over 7 years."

Tom responded. "Holy shit! Do they need a coach?!"

I think Tom knew at that point, that the Bruins weren't going to come close to what Cleveland was prepared to give me. But they didn't have to. I was ready to sign with Boston for the $100,000 a year if they offered it, but they never did. They never came close. I was ready to sign with the Crusaders.

A few days later I picked up Eddie Johnston in the morning and headed to a golf tournament. I made sure Eddie kept it between us, and let him know he should wait to sign with the Bruins, because I had been talking with Cleveland, and if I leave, he would have some nice leverage when he's negotiating. I had never seen Eddie so irate. He was steaming mad at me. When I asked about his reaction, he told me he'd just signed that morning. I told him that was okay, he would be in good shape in some form or fashion anyway.

I went back and forth with Cleveland trying to hammer out the details of the contract. In doing so, I called an attorney friend of mine, Nish Mascarin, to look over the particulars for me. He was my mother's lawyer back in St. Catharines.

In the end, I was very satisfied with the terms. They put my last year's salary of $250K in escrow so I could borrow off it, if I chose. I got a Lincoln Continental, money for a house, and even a clause in the contract that stated I would be paid even in time of war. It was a sweet deal.

Though Cleveland was meant to be more of a bargaining chip when negotiating with the Bruins, the terms of my contract suggested they were much more than that. I was about to embark on a future that did not so closely resemble my days in Boston. I was coming off another world championship with the Bruins, an organization motivated by its history, tradition, and heroes. And now I was part of a franchise that would be finding its way in professional hockey. My move to Cleveland, my contract, and its impact on everyone involved were symbolic of a couple of things: It was a new era in hockey, and more importantly, a new chapter in my life.

With the deal finally inked, it was time to go. In August 1972, my family and I packed up and headed to Cleveland. The kids were too young to notice the change in scenery. My wife was a pro, a rock, in the business of relocating to accommodate my changing employers. She had no problem at all with the move.

So I had a new home in a congenial district of Rocky River, on the west end of Cleveland. Most of the players ended up living in that area as well, so most of us were within a 10-mile radius.

I had a new boss, and the embrace of the local sports media and fans of the Crusaders. But before I could tighten my grip on this new reality, I developed a hemorrhoid problem that landed me right in the hospital. As it turned out, my new neighbor was a Jack Laskey. He was a doctor of anesthesiology and worked with Dr. Ray Rooney.

I was all set up. Rooney performed the operation. He cut out the hemorrhoid, put it on a gauze pad and showed it to me when he said, "Now here's a puck that got away." It was that big, and it represented my first day in Cleveland. I had to lie on my side in bed for the following three days. It was bittersweet. My first experience in Cleveland was coping with the extraction of the puck-size hemorrhoid! However, I did become very good friends with both Dr. Laskey and Dr. Rooney. They were terrific guys.

Now, technically speaking, I was still the property of the Bruins at this point. NHL contracts began on September 30th and obviously ran for a year, so a lot of us were prohibited from skating under the flag of the Crusaders until October 1st. However, under the leadership of Larry

Gordon (who, by the way, took a job running the merchandising for all of Nick Mileti's pro teams, including the Cavaliers, Crusaders, the Barons, and the Indians) we all got together and practiced for a couple of weeks as a unit. In those two weeks, I actually practiced as a forward in an effort to get in shape. Looking back, it was probably a fruitless attempt. Poor Bobby Whidden, the other goaltender under contract; he was in net for that brief time. Bobby and I became very good friends, as did our wives.

The lull also gave me and my new teammates time to get our feet wet socially, and explore the city. Saturday nights in Cleveland were as good as any I've been a part of as a professional hockey player. And that was a good thing. The problem was, we practiced on the east side of Cleveland, but a lot of the guys moved into neighborhoods on the west side, which was close to an hour's ride away. Suffice it to say, on many of those nights, it took me eight or nine hours to get home—when we decided to get together.

They were a good bunch of fellas on that team, whom I enjoyed hanging out with immensely. Truth be told, I only knew about three guys out of the gate when I joined the team: Skippy Krake, Ronnie Buchanan, and Gary Jarrett. Krake and Buchanan were in the Bruins organization with me. Gary Jarrett was actually an Ontario native who played for Rochester when I was in the Toronto organization.

The organization posted up at Bowling Green University for training camp. We had no coach, but a guy who worked for the league, Chuck Cato, the Director of Player Personal, who helped us out, along with an old pro named Billy Needham. Billy was one of the nicest guys I had ever had the pleasure of acquainting myself with in professional hockey. His nickname was "Silent Sam." He spent many years in the AHL as a defenseman for the Cleveland Barons, and would now take over the reigns as the Crusaders' head coach.

We practiced twice a day, at 9AM and 10PM, as that was the ice time that was available. The time slots made it difficult for us to head out late night and grab a few beers and be ready to go in the morning for the early session, so we started playing poker in the middle of the day.

Now, we had a lot of guys on the team who came from the East Coast League; guys who played poker between whistles, if you catch my drift. One fella was Blake Ball. His name was synonymous with toughness around professional hockey. He set all the records for penalty minutes, and ironically, was a policeman in the off season in Canada. Blake was a big, burly, lovable guy as a person; but he couldn't skate very well as a hockey player. I had no problems seeing the puck when he was in front of the net because no one wanted to jostle with him.

Big Blake shook up the coziness anytime he sat down at a poker game. One time Paul Andrea, probably the funniest guy I had ever met in pro hockey, said, "No trying to bluff Blake."

There were a few sharp poker players, but we played for peanuts. It was just for fun; to pass the time. It was a good opportunity to get to know everyone there.

So what was once an organization searching for the rudimentary building blocks, was now looking like a team that had built some comradeship; albeit, a few games of poker never hurt. What was more important was that we were ready to play hockey. Despite the fact that we began the year with a roster consisting primarily of minor league talent, we were a pretty talented bunch—and a colorful bunch.

We had a player named Jimmy McMasters. He came from the West Coast Hockey League (WCHL) and was billed as the next Bobby Orr. No pressure. When I first arrived at camp I had to chuckle to myself when I first saw him; his hair was combed the same as Bobby, and he had one roll of tape on his stick like Bobby. He kept asking me, "What's Bobby like? What's Bobby like?"

I said, "He's the best. He works hard…"

"Oh, okay."

One day, we were having a beer and I happened to mention that Bobby never wore socks when he skated. The skates, apparently, fit better to his feet without them. A couple of days later I noticed McMasters on the training table with about twenty blisters pulsating on both feet. I finally said to him, "Listen, Jimmy, there's only one Bobby Orr. You have to be yourself."

So, Jimmy seemed to have broken out of the masquerade he was kidding himself with.

We opened the season up against the Quebec Nordiques, coached by Rocket Richard. The 7PM start represented the first ever contest played in the WHA. All other games had dropped the puck at 7:30PM or later.

The rest is well chronicled.

WHA PART II

Our inaugural game itself was a 1–0 score until we put it away with an empty net goal in the closing seconds.

Paul Shmyr was a tough guy who came from the Chicago organization and signed with the Crusaders. I wasn't too familiar with his play, but on that night, all 3 stars belonged to Shmyr. He was all over the place, blocking shots and wreaking havoc from one end of the ice to the other. Paul turned out to be a terrific player. In fact, in later years I tried to get him to come to Boston to play for the Bruins. He would have loved playing there.

Paul and I ended up being very close friends along with Gerry Pinder.

Pinder was another former Blackhawk who migrated over to Cleveland.

Ralph Hopiavouri was a big, loveable, red-headed fellow from Ontario who wore #4 for the Crusaders. Ralph was pretty tough; always tried to gauge the puck. He really tried his ass off out there on the ice.

Minutes after the 2–0 season opener victory, a reporter approached me and asked, "What's the biggest difference between the NHL and WHA?"

I said, "The biggest difference is, when I look up and see #4 carrying the puck up the ice, it's Ralph Hopiavouri, not Bobby Orr."

My quote ended up in Sports Illustrated. When Ralph's parents saw the article, they proceeded to underline the quote and send it along to Ralph, as they believed it was in poor taste. But Ralph got a chuckle out of it. He was a good guy.

Jimmy McMasters was so nervous he never played in that first game. Not a shift. The hype was too intense and so was the game. Jimmy was just a kid, eighteen years old, so the coach elected not to play him.

In the locker room, after the game, we were celebrating the win when Jimmy approached me and said, "Do you mind if I ask you a question?"

"Sure, go ahead."

He asked me, "Did Bobby play regularly his first year?"

I got a kick out of that one, even knowing that this obsession of his with Bobby was probably going to hurt him in the long run.

So, the Crusaders' inaugural season got off to a great start, but like any other season at any level, we had our usual good times and bad, and everything in between.

In November of that year we traveled to Minnesota to take on the Saints. The game turned upside down when Jim Wiste, while sitting in the penalty box, got into a fight with some WHA employee. In seconds, our bench was cleared and a melee broke out. Brawls were second nature to a lot of the players, but Minnesota really got on us for this one. They were throwing all kinds of stuff at us, like chairs, cups, and anything they could get their hands on. Luckily, none of us got hurt. A couple of weeks later we had to travel back to Minnesota to play them again. The word was out that Jimmy Wiste was going to be arrested for inciting the brawl. So Jimmy wore a fake mustache in an attempt to thwart the authorities. It didn't work. At least, he didn't fool anyone.

No matter the circumstances, it was always tough to keep these guys from having a good time.

On a scheduled road trip, the team headed into Chicago on a Friday afternoon, to get ready for a Saturday night game. We got out in front of the hotel at around 4PM when Bill Needham shouts, "Eleven o'clock curfew!"

Guys were booing and hissing upon hearing the harsh news. We were all chomping at the bit now to get out and enjoy downtown Chicago by 5PM. Bill Needham whispers in my ear, "Tell 'em I'm just kidding."

So we all went out and had a good time that night.

The following night we faced off against the Chicago Cougars.

Our primary team color was purple. I'll never forget Larry Cahan, a defenseman for Chicago, when he said, "It's the Minnesota Vikings!"

We went about our business that year, on and off the ice. Like the previous years with the Bruins, these guys always made it a point to stick together after games and on days off—whether it was at a bar or social gatherings with our families.

I remember a friend of mine throwing a barbeque for us. On the menu included a nice, golden brown, tender roast beef. It was a great day, weatherwise, and everyone was having a good time. One of the players took a piece of beef, put some gravy on it, and started eating. When he finished, all that was left was the rim of the paper plate he was using. The gravy was soaked in the plate and he ate right through the cardboard.

Traveling with the Crusaders was much the same as it was with the Bruins. Cleveland was a professional organization, so we always stayed in big cities, and in most cases it was two to three days at a time. And just like back in the NHL, it gave us a chance to explore each destination, and revisit some of the previous stops in case we missed something. Or we could simply meet up with an old friend or teammate living in the area.

There was this one particular road trip where we landed in Philadelphia to take on the Blazers. Philly is a great city, a fun city with a lot to
offer, including one Derek Sanderson. Derek had signed with the Blazers
in 1972–73 for one year. So, when we cruised into The City of Brotherly
Love, Derek and I made it a point to get together.

Sanderson was a character. He was known for his toughness, and
flamboyant nature, but he was also a very good hockey player. One time
I met up with him in Philly, and I brought the "kid" with me, Jimmy
McMasters. Derek was taking us around in his Rolls-Royce from one
after-hours place to the next. It was a great time. Derek was a lot of fun.
McMasters was in awe.

If nothing else, the extended stays gave the team time to connect off
the ice and develop social unity. As a result, we were an above .500 team,
who had great chemistry.

When the regular season concluded the team finished 2nd behind
the New England Whalers. We played some great games against that New
England team, too. There were a lot of overtime games, and I remember
getting beat 1–0 in the old Boston Arena.

We played one game on Tuesday night, and one game on the following
Saturday night, but we had no ice in between, so we stayed there. I took
some of the boys down to some of my favorite bars on Revere Beach like
The Shipwreck and The Driftwood, and Eddie Mac's on the beach. We
toured the beach for three days. We won the Saturday game, so we felt
we discovered a new way to train.

It turned out that the Whalers and Crusaders had a pretty heated
rivalry, which added to the intensity of the games. More importantly,
nail-biting contests gave the league the attention and respect it may have
been lacking.

It wasn't a fluke that the Whalers finished ahead of everyone in the standings. New England had a great goaltender in Al Smith, and guys who could score like Larry Pleau and Tom Webster. They were poised, and ready for post-season play, as were the Crusaders.

We breezed through the 1st round of the playoffs, sweeping the Philadelphia Blazers in 4 games. In round 2 we faced New England. Though the games were close, we lost the series 4–1. The Whalers eventually went on to win the Avco World Trophy, which was the Stanley Cup equivalent in the NHL.

To sum up my first year in Cleveland, I would have to say nothing less than it was a great experience. I was on a good team, I met some great people, and, maybe just as significant, I was able to reconnect with some old buddies and spend time with them.

I fared well as the starting goaltender, and, in fact, at season's end, I led the league with a 2.84 GAA, and posted 32 victories.

The city of Cleveland embraced me personally, and the Crusaders as well.

That summer I stayed primarily in Cleveland, but retreated back to the New England area from time to time where I rented a cottage in Salem, New Hampshire, near Rockingham on Cobbett's Pond. The area fit me, especially considering Rockingham Park was one of the oldest and most reputable race tracks around. That season I purchased a handful of thoroughbreds. The horses ran well and we won a bunch of races; the venture was pretty successful.

The 1973–74 season opened with us traveling to take on Gordie Howe and the Houston Aeros. Half of the city of Detroit flew in on a 747 from Detroit to see Gordie play with his two sons, Mark and Marty. The excitement was short lived, as we shut out the Howe trio and the Aeros 2–0.

After the contest I went to a post-game party with a bunch of the guys, including Wayne Hillman, who came over from the Flyers that year. During the game, Wayne was in front of the net when I slipped and fell trying to field the puck. Guys from Houston took about five shots at Wayne off his chest, elbow, and leg, all while he was standing there, blocking the goal. At the party, I said to Wayne, "Hey, Mooner, seventy-nine more games of these."

"Get me out of here," he said.

But it was a pretty good year. Five of us, including myself, were elected to the All-Star team in '74. The game was held in Quebec, CA, where it was sold out. There was a pre-game dinner where everyone wore suits and ties, except the Cleveland Crusaders. Someone had the idea to display our dissimilarity from the rest of the league and wear tuxedos, so we did. We rented them, of course. The Crusaders' owner was in attendance, and was so impressed, he said to me, "You make sure I get the bill."

I said, "You're getting it anyway," in a lighthearted fashion.

1974 SUMMIT SERIES

That was a particularly unique year because a group comprising WHA players, including myself, was chosen to take on the Russians in the 1974 Summit Series. Unlike the '72 team, we weren't favored to win, despite the fact that guys like Bobby Hull and other stars around hockey were allowed to play. In '72, the NHL decided that any player who jumped leagues to the WHA was not invited to play. So, they decided to hog the roster, which, to this day, was wrong. Nevertheless, this was a heavily anticipated series.

The team trained in Edmonton for the series, but the games were in Quebec, Toronto, Winnipeg, and Vancouver.

I roomed with Mike Shakey Walton, an Ontario native who had attended St. Mike's with me.

Billy "Hinky" Harris was our coach. Harris was all over the place. He coached Team Canada, the Swedish national team, and the Ottawa Nationals. He also won three Stanley Cup championships with the Toronto Maple Leafs. But all of his Frequent Flyer miles weren't enough to derail the Russians.

Overall, we played pretty well for being an underdog team, but only came away with a record of 1–4–3. But we still went out there and whacked them around a bit. It was a good experience.

I read somewhere that one of the Russians said I was the best goalie they had ever faced, or something to that effect. I've never known a Russian to lie, so it must have been true.

It was unfortunate, though, but during game 2, which was played in Toronto, my father-in-law had a heart attack while in attendance. He passed away shortly after.

Season 3 in Cleveland seemed to have perhaps represented the beginning of the end for me as a Crusader, and for the organization itself. The problem was we just didn't see it yet.

We had a disappointing year, finishing in 2nd place behind New England once again, and posted a sub .500 record. We skidded into the playoffs where we met Houston in the quarter finals. We didn't play well, and were defeated by the eventual champs, 4–1 in the series.

My 4th year under contract with Cleveland was a miserable year. We weren't faring well in the standings, and, personally, I was having one of my worst years as a pro in net. When mid-season approached, management decided a change needed to be made. Our coach, John Hanna, was let go, and replaced by a guy named Jack Vivian.

To make matters worse, rumblings were heard all over that the league's financial stability was in question. Many of the franchise were on the verge of collapse, including the Cleveland Crusaders. And after just three and a half years as the beloved owner, Nick Mileti sold the team to a wealthy car dealer named Jay Moore.

Jay was a big hockey fan, but he just couldn't manage the team from an executive standpoint; not effectively anyway. The organization was running out of money, and, eventually, a lot of the players' checks started bouncing.

I took it upon myself to use the stipulated $200,000 I had in escrow to cover the guy's paychecks, or else we wouldn't have had a team.

Regardless, my days were near its end. I was taking more shots from management, including Jack Vivian, than my opponents on the ice. I was being blamed for the team's poor play, and advised that I should quit after the organization believed I let the team down. Vivian came to Cleveland from the college game, and had a difficult time handling certain situations at the pro level. That's putting it kindly. So, as a result, he used me as the scapegoat.

I had finally heard enough. I told management they didn't have to pay me anymore, and then I asked to be released. Abruptly, I was put on waivers.

Teams had 48 hours to claim me off the wire, or I'd be given my unconditional release. And the odds of any team looking to pick up a player with a 4-year, $200,000 annual salary contract, was impractical to say the least. In other words, it wasn't going to happen. Now, while I was waiting for my time to run out on my marriage with the WHA, and once I cleared waivers, I was free to sign with Boston.

I can't say I had no regrets. In 1974 The Bruins played the Flyers in the Stanley Cup final and lost 4–2. I went to a couple of the games, and couldn't help but think that was a series I would have loved to play in. Back then, the Boston-Philly games were pretty intense, and I always seemed to have good luck against the Flyers. Don't get me wrong, the Bruins' goalie, Gilles Gilbert, played terrific in the series, but that was a series where you had to know what to do to beat the Flyers, and I knew. You had to call their bluff, attack, and be physical. I ended up playing against them again in the future…beat them up pretty good, too.

Nonetheless, the WHA was a wonderful experience, and I'll always look back on my time in Cleveland fondly, with exception to my last year. I forged many friendships as a result of my time with the Crusaders, and for that, I'm grateful. I took particular enjoyment in watching all the young guys work their butts off, each one hoping to maintain his status as a professional hockey player. Yet my most memorable experience as a Crusader was our 2–0 victory over Houston in Gordie's first game with his two boys.

But the World Hockey Association offered more than just memories, especially for a lot of other guys. I played with a lot of terrific hockey players; guys who may have been career minor leaguers had the WHA not been formed. Bob Whidden, my counterpart in net, was a very good goaltender who may never have been noticed if it weren't for the ambition of a couple of American promoters, Dennis Murphy and Gary Davidson.

There were many others just like Bob Whidden, and most of them, like Bob, had an opportunity to double, and sometimes triple, their salaries just from making the jump to the WHA from minor league hockey. And anyone coming from the AHL all seemingly signed with the same crooked agent from the west coast, and had inked contracts that emulated each other. The agent was charging guys 10 percent of their salaries until the players caught wise; that kind of percentage was a sting.

The WHA finally met its demise in 1979, but not before merging four teams with the NHL, namely, the Edmonton Oilers, the New England Whalers, the Winnipeg Jets, and the Quebec Nordiques.

I packed my bags and headed to Boston to begin the next phase in my career in a familiar place.

This section is dedicated to the life and memory of our friend,

Al Ruele

You will be missed.

1926-2011

*"I sure hope
the puck left
our end."*

*"Come on ref,
let's get this
over with!"*

*"Coaches aren't supposed
to be this good looking."*

*"Those guys coming this way look
really mad at me for some reason."*

"Come on, Parkie, you can't block shots from there!"

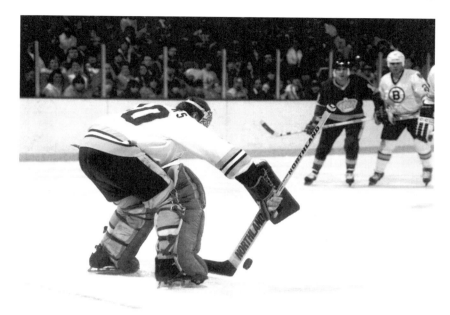

"I wish all saves were this easy."

"Hey, I really don't need this much help!"

"It's great to win."

"This is why we play."

BACK TO BOSTON

1975–1976

With my divorce from Cleveland final, and all moneys owed securely in the hands of both parties, I headed to Boston to return to my old job as goalie for the Bruins. I signed a 1-year deal for a little more than $200,000.

We bought a house, and resumed life in Boston like we never left.

However, now I had to get to know a lot of the new players, and of course, reacquaint myself with some of the guys who were there when I left, like Wayne Cashman, Gary Doak, Donny Marcotte, and Johnny Bucyk, to name a few. Then, there were the new guys…to me, anyway.

What roster spots were once taken up by Stanley Cup champions were still occupied by some pretty terrific hockey players, like Terry O'Reilly and Rick Middleton. But that season was marked perhaps by the blockbuster trade that sent Phil Esposito to the New York Rangers in exchange for defenseman Brad Park and forward Jean Ratelle. By the time I got back, however, Phil was already gone.

After practicing for three days with the team, I realized I was more prepared to test flight a shuttle to the moon than I was to play in my first NHL game in four years. So, on a road trip that started in Toronto, I found myself on the bench, backing up rookie goaltender, Dave Reece.

It was that particular game when Daryl Sitler of the Maple Leafs tallied 6 goals and 4 assists, setting a record for most points in a game by a player in NHL history. It was tough to find me on the bench that night. I slid down one spot after every Sitler goal. I wanted no part of that. Then coach, Don Cherry, nicknamed Grapes, left Reece in until the buzzer sounded.

I felt bad for Reece. We were on a charter headed back to Boston the following night, when I told our trainer, Frosty, to sit with me in the back of the plane so I could hide from Don Cherry; I wanted Reece to get to start against the Red Wings back home. They weren't a very good team, and I felt he needed to get back in there to restore some confidence. We got off the plane and began trekking through the airport. I thought I was in the clear, until Grapes jumped out from behind a pole like a croc surprising a wilder beast. He said, "You're playing tonight, no ifs, ands, buts about it."

The other goalie was Gilles Gilbert, but he was hurt at the time.

I said, "Okay."

I wasn't ready to play, so when we got in that night I told Frosty I needed a couple of beers to get loose and get a good night's sleep. I did. The day of the game I headed to the arena early. I was a little anxious. The move back to Boston was surreal, and again, I felt I wasn't ready for game speed just yet. But in the end, my concerns had seemed to be an exercise in futility, as we beat Detroit in my first game back by a score of 7–0.

The win jumpstarted good play in the team, and me, as well, as I went unbeaten in my first 10 or 12 starts. I only got in 15 games that year for Boston, so overall I played pretty well in my abbreviated season with the B's.

We had a very good regular season, and when it ended, we were crowned Adams Division champions. The triumph earned us a 1st round bye in the playoffs.

After defeating the L.A. Kings in 7 games, we faced off against the Philadelphia Flyers.

The Flyers were coming off a Stanley Cup championship the year before. And with a lot of the same guys back on their roster, they were pretty stout again, and it showed.

I split time in net with Gilles Gilbert throughout, and although I played pretty well, we couldn't get past them that year. It had been some time since I last had the pleasure of facing them; this wasn't the "welcome back" party I was looking forward to.

It was a bitter end to a topsy-turvy season mixed with extraordinary headlines, the comings and goings of some terrific hockey players, and, of course, my re-indoctrination into the NHL. But, luckily, next year was another campaign, and another opportunity to make some noise in the post season.

That summer was underscored again with racing at Rockingham, and gradually becoming more and more inundated with the yearning to play golf.

1976–1977

When the 1976–77 season began, I was pretty excited; I felt really good physically, and knowing we had a very talented team returning, made it all the better.

But, by the time the season began, Bobby Orr was the property of the Blackhawks. It was the result of some arduous negotiations between the Bruins and Orr's agent, Alan Eagleson. In the end, Bobby signed with Chicago. So, whereas a lot of guys from the Cup-winning years were still there, the face of the team had changed.

Grapes returned as our head coach. As a coach, he wasn't a great x's and o's guy, but he was fundamentally sound. His thing was, get the puck in and take the body. It was simple, and I thought a very good approach to managing a game. Grapes' philosophy was a tremendous influence on why we were so successful during this period.

With Don always came some excitement. I had a horse, a stallion named "Royal Ski," who was running in a $250,000 race in Philadelphia on a Saturday. It was a long awaited off-day for us. So, I had made arrangements for my wife and me to attend the race. We had reservations at a hotel. We were going to stay overnight, then come back home early, so I'd be on time for Sunday's game. I had it all figured out until Grapes changed the practice time from 10am to 2pm. I needed a plan.

The day before the race, I worked my butt off in practice. Grapes was scratching his head, probably wondering why. I told our trainer, Frosty, to wait for Don to mosey over to within a few feet of me, then ask me if I'm going to the big race tomorrow. When Grapes was close, I gave Frosty the nod, and he came through perfectly. Frosty said, "Cheese, you going to the big race tomorrow?"

I said, "No, I can't, we have practice at 2."

Grapes intervened. "What big race?"

I said, "Oh, Royal Ski is favored in a $250,000 race."

"You're not going?" Grapes asked with great surprise.

I said, "No, you changed practice."

"That's why you're working so hard today!" Grapes went on. "You go ahead. You worked hard today."

"No, no," I told him. With a touch of sarcasm, I continued, "Hockey is my #1 priority, I would never do that."

"You go ahead, don't worry."

During this time, Grapes and Harry were feuding a bit. So, I asked him, "What's Harry going to say about it?" That didn't faze him at all.

"I'm ordering you to go!"

He made me go, and I was okay with that.

The weekend turned out great. My wife and I had a terrific time, and Royal Ski won the race.

Royal Ski was a great horse, my best horse, in fact. He should have been awarded "Two-Year-Old of the Year," but he got beat out by Seattle Slew. At that time, Royal Ski was the third-leading two-year-old winner of all time.

That same year he was victorious in another race, this one in Laurel Park, just outside Washington, D.C. To boot, we had a game that night against the Canadiens. Grapes thought I was so excited about the race that I wouldn't care, and take a lax approach to the game against the Canadiens. He wasn't going to play me.

I told him, "You don't play me, I'm quitting."

I played, and it was one of the few times we won up there in Montreal. After the game I talked to a few of the Canadiens, including Serge Savard, who said to me, "As soon as we heard your horse won that day, we figured you were going to beat us tonight."

Although I did miss a lot of races during the hockey season, that was okay. I got the updates. I remember Wayne Cashman being quoted in Sports Illustrated as saying, "Horseracing has the Vanderbilts, the Whitneys, and the Cheeverses." It was humorous, and a testament to my involvement in the sport.

Gilles Gilbert and I, again, were the goalies in 1976–77. I had a very good regular season, winning 30 games and only losing 10, with 5 ties.

When the regular season concluded, we barely squeaked by, winning the division by 2 points over the Buffalo Sabres. Nonetheless, the title would give us a break before beginning another march toward a Stanley Cup championship.

We beat the Kings 4–2 in the quarter finals, then, along came the Flyers.

Philly had just come off a 4–2 series win against the Toronto Maple Leafs, winning two games in overtime.

The Flyers series was particularly notable because, ironically, we won a pair of overtime games in Philly, including one in double overtime. It was a cruel twist of fate handed to the "Broad Street Brawlers." But we'd take it. Terry O'Reilly had one game winner, and Rick Middleton had the other. We put the Flyers on ice when we swept the series 4–0.

The sweep would indicate we had an easy time of it, but truth be told, it was a tough, physical, hard fought series. The Flyers were a talented bunch with guys like Bobby Clarke, Bill Barber, and Rick MacLeish, and they had a terrific goaltender in Bernie Parent. It was no wonder they were a perennial post-season threat.

One of my fondest memories in hockey came in game 4 of that series. We were winning 3–0 with about 5 minutes to go, when Bobby Clarke came bearing down on me. I let the puck drop so he would come and get it. I wanted to stick him pretty good. But Clarke slammed on the brakes and said, "It's all over, Cheese."

Bobby Clarke was fierce on the ice. He wouldn't admit it, but he'd take your eye out if he had to. And he was famous for sticking guys, then apologizing for it. So in a brief moment, when he succumbed to the defeat, it was special.

I was really on top of my game in that series, and I loved playing in Philly. My play against the Flyers and the series outcome reinforced my thoughts, that, had I not gone to Cleveland, I would have played in the Cup finals against the Flyers. And I believe the outcome would have been more favorable for Boston.

Unfortunately, in a reversal of fortune, we were swept by the Montreal Canadiens in the finals that same year.

Sweeping the Flyers was fitting, but sadly, almost just as fitting, it was another season we felt we could have won the Cup, and did not.

1977–1978

We had every reason to feel optimistic the following season. The fact that we experienced defeat at the hands of our now bitter rivals, the Canadiens, did not diminish the talent we had on our roster, or the drive to win a championship.

But, whereas our team was poised for another run toward post-season play, personally, I had to stutter-step my way to the finish line. I had some aches and pains, and sat out most of the season, getting in just 21 games. That particular year, Ron Grahame, a top-notch goaltender who came over from the WHA, played a lot of games for us, and played pretty well. Ronnie was a great individual; a good person.

This was a different era in Bruins hockey. No longer were we identified by the transcendent talents of Bobby Orr, or the prolific scorers like Phil Esposito and Johnny McKenzie. This team was tough, balanced, and played as a unit. The blue collar approach hit such a high note around hockey we were nicknamed the "Lunch Pail Gang."

The system worked. That year the Bruins had 11 guys with 20 or more goals. It was a feat our coach, Don Cherry, took great pride in.

We rolled to the top of the Adams Division, once again outlasting the runner up Sabres for the second year in a row.

In the quarterfinals we met the Blackhawks. Bobby was still a member of Chicago, but sat out the entire 1977–78 season due to an injury. The Blackhawks certainly could have used him, as we swept the series 4–0.

In the semifinals, our familiar foes, the Philadelphia Flyers, rolled into town.

During the 1970s, the Flyers won two Stanley Cups and wreaked havoc in the post season every other year. This series made sense, and so did the outcome. We took them 4–1, and advanced to the Cup finals to once again meet the Montreal Canadiens.

In that series against the Flyers, Ronnie Grahame got the start in game 3 at Philadelphia, a tough spot for the young goaltender. I said, "Ronnie, the only tip I can give you is, you have to be aggressive against these guys. They'll eat you up in front of the net if you let them. Use your stick to your advantage."

We lost 2–1, but Ronnie played a great game. On the plane back to Boston, Ronnie asked me, "What happens if you keep sticking them, and they keep coming back?"

I told him, "Stick them harder, and stick them where it really hurts."

That was the only way to command presence in front of the net against those guys. Nonetheless, it was off to Montreal. We knew this would be a battle.

We dropped the first 2 games in Montreal, including a 3–2 overtime loss in game 2. That overtime session was one of the best periods of hockey I had ever played. I must have made at least 15 saves in 10 or 12 minutes, until Guy Lafleur came down the right wing. I cheated toward the other side, thinking he was going to pass, but he took a slap shot and scored, short side. It was a great shot by him, but a terrible play by me.

But we battled back, winning the next two games in Boston.

Unfortunately, that was it, though. We lost the final two games of the series, each by the score of 4–1, thus taking a back seat to the Habs one more time.

1978–1979

That off season was like any other. I filled my time with horse racing and golf, family getaways, and impromptu fun with hockey buddies. Previously, I had joined the Indian Ridge Country Club in Andover, Massachusetts. It was just a gorgeous place, with a very impressive 18-hole course. It was built in the early sixties, so it was relatively new at the time. We made a lot of great friends at the club. Despite my commitment to leisure, as it seemed, I trained, too, to ready myself for another year with the Bruins.

The outlook for the 1978–79 season was promising as always. Some of the younger guys like Rick Middleton, Peter McNab, and Terry O'Reilly were really coming into their own. And though by hockey standards I would be considered ensconced in my twilight years, I could still handle the arduous grind an NHL season had to offer. Gilles Gilbert was a terrific complement to the tandem, and that season, Jim Pettie came up from Rochester and got a few starts in net and played pretty well.

That particular year was the first in many when the NHL All-Star game was not played. Instead, players from the Soviet Union team headed to North America, and faced off against NHL players in a 3-game series called the Challenge Cup. The Russians won the series 2–1.

I played in the 3rd game and didn't play well at all. The final score was 6–0, in favor of the Soviets.

When the NHL resumed play, we cruised to the top of the division again, outlasting the Buffalo Sabres, this time by 12 points.

After the bye, we were matched up against the Penguins in a best of 7. We played to a couple of one-goal games, but in the end, we swept Pittsburgh 4–0.

The series sweep meant we were ready for post-season play that year, but not for what was about to happen next.

Our next opponent was the Canadiens. We were down in the series 3 games to 2 when we put together a great effort, beating the Habs 5–2, and forcing a game 7 in Montreal.

Early in that series I overextended my knee and ripped the outside ligament. I tried playing through it, but I wasn't effective. So, Gilbert went in and did a great job.

But it was game 7 when we made the most critical error, at the most critical time. With a 4–3 lead late in the contest, the referee called us for 'too many men on the ice.' We were given a 2-minute minor with just a few minutes left in the game. Guy Lafleur tied the game on the power play, sending it into overtime. In the extra session, Yvon Lambert would score the game winner for the Canadiens.

It was a crushing defeat for the franchise, and for the fans. It was so demoralizing it cost Don Cherry his job, and it left the rest of the team scratching our heads. We couldn't help but begin to wonder if we could ever beat that team. We knew we were every bit as talented as Montreal, each and every time we played them. It just didn't happen for us. In the end, we always came up on the short end of the score, or series.

Thank God, since then, the Bruins eventually beat the Habs in the post season, and on several occasions.

1979–1980

After Grapes was let go, the organization hired Fred Creighton, a guy who had had a very successful coaching career that spanned fifteen years.

Five of those were spent as the head coach of the NHL's Atlanta Flames (before the franchise moved to Calgary).

That particular year was unique because the NHL had now made it mandatory for players to wear helmets. The only exceptions were for the guys who signed contracts before June 1, 1979. For them, it was optional. For me, it meant nothing. My only focus was to get ready for the pre season.

The exhibition season is meant to get loose, to work out any kinks that may have manifested over the warm summer months on the golf course, or whatever activity other than hockey one would partake in. It was a time to get back into playing shape, to get ready for the 9-month haul that was ahead. But when we faced off against the Philadelphia Flyers that year in a pre-season game, it was something else.

It was a typical Bruins-Flyers brawl night when Terry O'Reilly and Behn Wilson kicked it off with one of the best fights I had ever seen in hockey. These guys were two very tough individuals. They threw 500 punches, or so it seemed. I think they fought in every period. The fight actually carried into the stands. Some of us lost the edge of our skates, so when the 2nd period began, we were four men short.

I was sitting there with Bernie Parent, hanging out, when Billy Barber grabbed me from behind and shouted, "I got him! I got him!"

"Billy," I said. "I'm with Bernie."

We laughed and he took off.

I'll say this: The Flyers may have been nicknamed "The Broad Street Bullies," but they never bullied the Boston Bruins. They never pushed us around, far from it.

We fit in perfectly with the rough and tumble terrain of the NHL with some of the toughest guys in hockey. At times, some of them couldn't wait to prove it. I remember a night when Pittsburgh rolled into town.

They had a player named Kim Clackson, maybe the toughest little guy you'd ever see in your life; you couldn't hurt him. I remembered him from my days in the WHA when he played for the Indianapolis Racers, so I knew. I heard the murmurs in the locker room. Things like, "How does he fight?" Or, "Is he left-handed?" I told our guys, "You don't want to fight this guy." I thought it would be a shame to lose one of our guys to a fight with him. They didn't listen. Someone was going to have a piece of him. Stan Jonathan fought him twice, and Al Secord dropped the gloves as well. Both Jonathon and Secord got the better of Clackson. It was one of those nights.

Lurking below the radar that particular season were the New York Islanders. They were a talented bunch, but posted a modest regular season record and finished behind the Flyers for the top spot in the Patrick Division. They looked like a team on the rise.

We had some heroic battles with the Islanders that season, mainly due to the penalty minutes we racked up by way of dropping the gloves. In a game late in that year, Wayne Cashman squared off with Garry Howatt in one of the great fights of all time. No sooner did one fight end, another one would break out. O'Reilly got into it a couple of times with Clark Gillies; Mike Milbury and Stan Jonathan both had a piece of someone. But it was Wayne Cashman and Garry Howatt who had one of the great fights of all time. Howatt was a very tough guy and so was Cash. The fight was epic.

Billy Smith was the goalie for the Islanders. We're friendly today, but that night Billy wanted to fight me. His words said one thing, but his eyes told something else. They rolled back a bit, so I declined. I said to Billy, "Whoa, kid, back off!"

"Come on, Cheese," he said. "We're supposed to fight."

"No," I said.

I didn't want to fight a goaltender anyway.

The "Isles" other goaltender was Glenn "Chico" Resch. I paired up with Chico and just shot the breeze for a bit.

Gilles Gilbert was actually a great fighter, but he and Billy Smith never connected. That would have been a great fight.

Finally, the season would begin, and it was that season that I got my first glimpse of one Raymond Bourque. I knew right off the bat that Ray was going to be a terrific player. He was strong, powerful, and worked really hard. He looked every bit like the player the scouts and everyone else were touting. As the season went on, he began proving it. Ray had an outstanding rookie season.

Gilles and I continued to split time in net, and statistically, we both had very good years. And though we finished with 105 points that year, we couldn't catch the streaking Sabres, and when the season concluded, we found ourselves finishing in 2nd place behind Buffalo.

We didn't play well down the stretch. In fact, the 2nd half of the season was marred by inconsistent play, and we were essentially playing .500 hockey. This allowed the Sabres to take control of the division.

If that wasn't enough of a wake-up call, with just 7 games remaining on the schedule, the organization fired Creighton as our head coach. Harry Sinden, who was our GM at the time, filled in and went 6–1 to close the regular season.

We opened up the playoffs against Pittsburgh. After dropping 2 of the first 3 games, we really turned it on by scoring 14 goals in the final 2 games, and winning the series, 3 games to 2. Next up was the New York Islanders.

The Islanders were a very talented club. They had some great goal scorers like Bryan Trottier and Mike Bossy. Billy Smith and Chico Resch were very good goaltenders.

However, we weren't intimidated by any stretch—just frustrated.

We dropped the first 2 games in overtime at our place. That set the tone. After going down 3–0, we managed to win a game in New York, before falling in game 5 and losing the series.

The Islanders would go on to win the Stanley Cup, which began an impressive run of 4 championships in as many years. I suppose if we took solace in anything, it's that it seemed every team that ever beat us in the playoffs went on to win the Cup. But the thought wasn't enough to pick us back up—ever.

That summer my knee was really bothering me, so I went to see our team doctor, Dr. Zarins, to get an opinion. I was thirty-nine years old, and honestly felt, if it hadn't been for the knee, I could have played another ten years. That's how much I loved the game. But Dr. Zarins told me that there was no way he could get me ready for another season just by scoping my knee. He said, "I'm going to have to open you up, and do a good job of cleaning you up and tightening things down there." I had had enough surgeries. I didn't want another one.

In '78 I sold a horse for a nice piece of change, so I had some money, and it really played a part in my decision making. I was done.

I was at peace with my decision. I would miss playing, but I had been a hockey player for nearly forty years of my life. I met so many wonderful people, and compiled so many terrific memories, that I decided it was enough.

I was fortunate enough to play on a couple of championship teams with a great bunch of guys. We had such chemistry. It was things like that I would miss the most. More than anyone, though, I enjoyed the company of Wayne Cashman. He was so unpredictable, and he may never have been depicted this way, but I would describe Cash as a very bright individual. He was an intellectual. Some of the best writers and reporters in the world had trouble deciphering the words he delivered after an interview. I had a lot of great teammates over the years, but Cash was the very best I ever had.

I had no regrets, only a wish that we had won a couple more Stanley Cups, something I knew we were capable of doing. To do that, it meant we'd have to beat the Canadiens on those quests. If I had a change of heart, and wanted to lace up the skates one more time, it would be for those two reasons; to win the Cup, and beat Montreal in the process. But I had no such sentiment. After twenty-one years as a pro, I decided to call it quits.

I walked into Harry Sinden's office one day and said, "Harry, I've decided to retire. If I try to play, I might have to sit out as many as three months after I'm cut open. I can't be scoped this time."

That was it. There was no final skate around the Garden for the fans, or a tearful goodbye to the media. In fact, I wasn't even sure when I took the ice for the final time that it was going to be the last time I ever put on a uniform.

Harry said, "Okay." He never argued the point, but in the same breath he went on, "You have until next Friday to make a decision and let me know if you want to coach the team or not."

I had a week to decide, but, truthfully, I had no idea he was going to ask such a thing, and I never had any inclination of even entertaining the thought before I met Harry that day. So, in the following week I did a lot of thinking. I consulted with my family and friends, and weighed the positives and negatives.

COACHING

Mentally, I was as strong as ever, however, my body felt something else. It couldn't go on. It wouldn't even try. I wouldn't let it. And though a lot of athletes in my position struggle with the realization their playing career must cease, sometimes too abruptly, I was at peace with my decision.

The game—and all it offered on and off the ice—was great to me. I valued the awards and recognition, and the relationships I forged along the way, some of which continue to prosper to this day. All of this and becoming a world champion twice with a tremendous group of individuals meant the most to me.

Now, conversely, I was to take a hard right into retirement, away from the game that nurtured me the better part of my life. I would hit the links and do it often. My golf game was on the ups. I would plan family vacations, weekend outings with the "boys," and sit back and enjoy my newfound restful and unhurried activities. That was my plan. No grieving. No regrets. No second thoughts about returning to hockey. Let another phase of my life begin. That was until one Friday afternoon when Harry so bluntly offered me the Boston Bruins head coaching job.

I felt shock, and some mystification. After all, I had no "real" coaching experience aside from teaching drills to youngsters in hockey camps, or giving pointers to goaltenders my junior. But my reaction did not afford me much, as I had a mere one week to decide, and I needed it. But before the week was up, I accepted the job.

The first order of business was to accept the fact that my salary would be slashed by something close to 60 percent. It was a terrible cut in pay, but it truly didn't bother me. But something would, later, as the job progressed.

Now, I'd become the fifteenth coach in Bruins' history. A job held in high esteem across hockey. From guys like Art Ross, the first coach of Boston's illustrious past and first boss to win a Stanley Cup, to Harry Sinden, a great coach and Stanley Cup winner himself. These coaches—and all those in between—left their mark in the Boston Garden leading the black and gold, and now it was my turn.

To better equip myself mentally for the challenge I reached out to different people and coaches, including Al Arbour, who was the head of the New York Islanders at the time. Al was a great coach, a good friend, and a trusted comrade. I first met him in Rochester when he was my captain for the AHL's Americans. Now he led an extremely talented Islanders team that won the Stanley Cup championship the previous year. Al gave me the ins and outs, the fine points, as well as what chain of circumstances to expect. And the first would be the hardest.

I had to get used to coaching guys who were my teammates just a few months before. It was surreal, and I had a feeling I would have a tough time dealing with it in the years to come. Moreover, I was now out of the players' circle. They did their thing and I did mine.

Though I made my living as a goaltender for twenty-one years as a pro, I never took supplementary interests in the goalies. There were some guys along the way who could have used some extra tutoring, including Mike Moffat. He played well in a 7-game series in 1983, but he was a guy I felt could have used the help. But we had a lot of young goalies in Mike's position. It would have been tough. I had to cast a big net so I could focus on the task of being their head coach. Unfortunately, goalie coaches hadn't been recognized as an official job on NHL teams until a few years later.

Nonetheless, I adapted well to life as a coach. After all, I inherited a talented team, which always makes it easy for a new skipper coming in. Guys like Rick Middleton, Brad Park, Peter McNabb, and Wayne Cashman were all terrific hockey players, and all returned that season to the Bruins. Suffice it to say, I understood the roster well, who could do what, where we were strong, and where we needed help. But the players now had to understand a new coach.

Don Cherry loved to yell. He rode the refs, sometimes a bit too much, but that was his personality. I don't believe we ever got the best of it. The recently departed Fred Creighton hardly ever said a word. That effect was negative also. Vocally, my approach was somewhere between the two. That included what was said in the locker room. There weren't too many, "Win one for the Gipper," speeches, but at the same time I was seldom short on words. Grapes, Harry Sinden, and Father Bauer were all great pre-game speakers in their own way. It's not an easy task to find the right words and give guys the slight edge needed to get up for a contest. More than words, though, coaching runs deeper, and finding a winning approach never ceases to be challenging.

Grapes had his own strategy for winning, though, and that was this: Get it in and get it out. Keep 'em off the boards and you're probably going to win. That was his sentiment and it worked. He needed a physically tough group of guys to execute his philosophy and he found it in guys like Terry O'Reilly, Stan Jonathan, Wayne Cashman, and Al Secord. With those guys, if they shoot the puck around the boards in their own zone, it usually got out pretty easily.

As far as x's and o's, well, I always believed you had to forecheck to win. Keep the other team from doing what they wanted to do. That was my thing. Of course, between learning from guys like my dad and Vic Teal, and playing pro hockey most of my life, I picked up a lot that would help me as a coach. It also never hurt that I had played under some of the game's greatest coaches, guys like Joe Crozier, Harry Sinden, Grapes, and Father Bauer, my juniors' coach. However, I never emulated any one coach; I just took a little from all my experiences and transferred what I thought worked for me to the bench.

The pre season was upon us, and it seemed to come quicker this time. I remember an exhibition game against the Flyers. It was Mike Keenan's first year as head coach, and he turned out to be a pretty good coach over time.

It began as a typical Bruins-Flyers match-up when fights broke out in the first period. Once those were out of the way, we played some hockey. But Keenan was matching lines every step of the way, which caused massive delays in the game. Between the gloves being dropped and Keenan's slow tactics, it took nearly two hours to finish the first period. In the hallway after the period ended I saw Mike.

"Mike!"

"Yeah," he said.

"Would you mind telling me who you want on the ice so we can get this thing over with?"

One of my favorite players was a guy who didn't even have a contract my first year. His name was Bobby Schmautz. Bobby was a well-traveled professional, a tough and gritty veteran, who had seemingly found a home with the Bruins, signing with Boston in 1974 and playing a span of more than five years with the organization.

When training camp opened my first year as head coach, Bobby Schmautz was unsigned, but was negotiating with the Bruins. So I tried to give Bobby as much time on the ice as I could during our exhibition season. But it was to no avail. He never came to terms with Boston, and since a deal never materialized, Schmautz went on to play elsewhere.

Though Bobby was gone, the chemistry and identity of the team remained intact. Along with our physical style of play, we had a group of very good hockey players like Brad Park, Jean Ratelle, and a young, rising star named Ray Bourque who I played with just a season ago.

Ray was a quiet kid, but a good kid and a great hockey player. He came with big expectations and fulfilled them all.

We acquired Jim Craig via trade with the Calgary Flames. Craig was still riding the coattails of his superb play in the 1980 Olympics when the U.S. won the gold. What the U.S. did in those Olympics was the single greatest hockey achievement in this country's history, and Jim was a big part of it. So, naturally, wherever Craig went, he would be the focal point of the team. It was no different when he came to Boston. There was considerable hype surrounding the young goalie when he made his way back to his home state of Massachusetts. But the glory he found in international play had escaped his grasp in the National Hockey League. Craig was a young man who was very sure of himself.

At times Jim was attacked by the media. He was put in some situations where his intentions (and what he wanted to say) versus what he actually said, were two very different things. As a result, Jim unwittingly put his teammates in some difficult spots.

That season, though, began promising enough, at least after one game. The first game in my professional coaching career was a victory. The subsequent eight or ten games were terrible. We went on quite a losing streak, and I felt I had no idea what I was doing.

We were in St. Louis one game and we were dreadful. So I got the team up at 8AM for a practice with no pucks. I had them skate for 90 minutes. It was brutal. But we worked it out. The team eventually played much better.

I had played with or knew most of the guys on the team, including Bourque, as a result of playing in the NHL. As much as I enjoyed their company in past years, I was their coach now, and that truth alone was arduous to deal with, especially when I had to sit a player; sometimes it was a guy I had probably gone to war with. Cash, Donny Marcotte, and Gary Doak were all nearing the end of their playing days, and scratching them from the lineup from time to time was as uncomfortable as I've ever felt, especially when they disagreed with my decision. Most of the time that was the case. These guys were tough competitors, as was I, so at least I knew how they felt.

I called Al Arbour and asked him what he felt was the best way to handle that type of situation. Al said, "Give them the lineup. If they have anything to say about it, tell them to come and see you the following day." They usually cooled off by then.

I didn't like it, and it was probably what I hated most about coaching. However, I had to be fair to the system and everyone involved, and, most importantly, the players. Unfortunately, relationships I greatly valued at one time had become strained.

As it was, we managed to finish in second place, modestly, with 87 points behind the Buffalo Sabres. Right there with us were the Minnesota North Stars, our eventual first-round opponent.

It was evident that season that the Stars were tired of being pushed around. They came into the league in '67 and had little success since. This year, they had a pretty good team, though. Their coach was Glen Sonmor. Glen, with his glass eye, was quite a character. He was a passionate guy, full of vigor and emotion.

Minnesota rolled into town and really challenged us one night. There must have been 20 fights that night, but that wasn't important. What was important was the score; we beat them that game pretty handily. The Stars just wanted to fight that night, and that's what they got.

We'd face them again, of course, when the playoffs began.

It was ugly. We didn't play well at all until the last half of the 3rd period in game 3, but by that time, the series was lost. I remember their manager, Louie Nanne, coming in to say to us, "I'm glad the series didn't go any longer."

"Louie," I said. "Get the fuck out of here, will ya?"

They had us right from day one, or game one.

The loss was painful. You never want to go out in round 1, let alone exiting by way of a sweep. The defeat was particularly bothersome for me because I was used to winning. It's what I hated most about coaching. Very seldom did any team I played on find themselves eliminated so quickly, and so decisively. But a cold hard fact is that there can only be one winner in this thing. The year began with 21 teams, 20 of which had failed, and were reluctantly ensconced on the golf courses. By the outset, only one team would hoist the Cup, and it was not us. The only thing we could do was look to improve the following year.

In my second year as head coach, much to my delight, the Bruins hired a pair of assistant coaches, former players in Jean Ratelle and Gary Doak, who took a lot of the burden away from me. Both guys were terrific coaches. Doak was especially good with the defensemen. Jean was simply a class act. I was fortunate enough to be a teammate of his for a handful of years. To be able to coach him the previous year was just a dream.

So, we had a talented bunch of players, and a solid coaching staff. The season began with us playing well; we were on our way.

We returned home to Boston on a road trip, however, and I wasn't feeling well. I was over Harry Sinden's house for dinner on a Saturday night when I felt great discomfort in my abdomen. As it turned out, I needed an emergency appendectomy. We had a game the following day on Sunday, but I never made it. In fact, I missed the next ten days or so due to the surgery. Harry took over behind the bench with Doakie and Ratelle, while I was doing some directing from my bed.

I eventually made it back, and by season's end we finished in 2nd place behind the Canadiens. We defeated the Sabres in the first round by a 3–1 margin in games. In the division finals we were engaged in a tough series with the Nordiques. We took the first 2 games, but Quebec won the next 3. The series eventually went 7 when we lost a heartbreaker 2–1 at the Garden.

Two years and a pair of disappointing endings wasn't my style. We needed to improve.

The following year marked the end of a brilliant career for Wayne Cashman. He had announced his retirement. Brad Park's tenure with the Bruins ended when he signed with the Detroit Red Wings at the conclusion of the 1983 post season.

The team's video coach was Joe Culhane. He was a delight, one of the guys. I wasn't too well versed in the rules and regulations surrounding videotaping, when and why we were doing it. Apparently after every game the home team is to supply the visiting team with the video recording of the contest between the two. It was a reciprocal rule across the board. That being said, I recall a game against the Vancouver Canucks in the Garden. It was a make-up as the result of a snowed-out game. Roger Neilson, the Canucks' head coach, who was the guru of game tapes, couldn't wait to get his hands on the reel for that game. Unfortunately for Neilson, the last episode of M.A.S.H. was airing that night, so we had other ideas on what we wanted to record. I knew we weren't going to see Vancouver again until the following year, so I had Joe tape, "Goodbye, Farewell and Amen," which was the name of the show's finale.

Immediately following the game, we all huddled around the TV to watch the show when Joe came in said, "Their coach is up there. He wants the video."

"Tell him we haven't got it," I said.

"No, he demands it. It's a deal," he said. He then referred to rule so and so, explaining why we had to share the game tapes.

"Okay," I said. "I'll go talk to him."

I didn't have the nerve to tell him I taped M.A.S.H. instead. I didn't want him to have a fit, so I told him I'd grab a copy from Channel 38 and send it to him.

I was never a big videotape guy. Quite honestly, I wasn't any good at watching them, and coming to any conclusion at the outcome of a play. Doakie was, though. He'd look at them for hours. He knew what he was doing.

As far as the game went that night, we put on a clinic. Vancouver had maybe 8 shots on net, which probably compounded Neilson's frustrations. After I spoke with him, I joined my team and finished watching the show. Ironically, the 'Nielsen' rating, as it's spelled, measures the audience in mass to estimate how many people tune in to watch any given show. To no one's surprise, that night M.A.S.H. got a lot of play. That night also proved to be a moment of levity I'll never forget.

Both Park and Cashman played well in their final seasons with the Bruins, and the team itself finished atop the Adams Division with 110 points, 12 points ahead of the second-place Canadiens. Pete Peeters won the Vezina Trophy as the league's best goaltender. We had every reason to be optimistic, as we saw ourselves advancing to the Conference Finals to play against the three-time Stanley Cup champions—the New York Islanders.

Despite finishing in 2nd place in their division, New York was still very formidable, and it showed. The Islanders scored 8 goals twice on us, and put up 7 in game 3. We ended up losing in 6. Again, I slept like a baby that night.

The following season seemed as though we were readying ourselves for another run at the Cup. We finished in first in the division with 104 points. Montreal had the worst record of any playoff team in our Prince of Whales Conference. We drew the Canadiens in the first round, and like a reoccurring nightmare, Montreal swept us out of the playoffs 3–0.

It was getting old, and to have been the man at the helm for four years now without winning a championship is to wonder where I'd be the following year.

When spring turned to summer, I was still the coach of the Bruins, so I knew, at least for now, when the season opened, it would commence with me on the bench calling the shots.

But for how long?

We had just played a home-and-home series against Chicago, Thursday and Sunday. We lost both games by a goal; both heartbreakers. I knew it was over then. I knew it was coming. From there we were on our way to Los Angeles for the all-star break. Harry and other management types went to L.A. as well, but not for the game. I remember being in my hotel room and realizing there were 150 phone messages on the machine from various radio stations and other media outlets. They were all looking for a quote in response to my possible firing.

So I caught up with Harry only to hear him say, "My worst fears have become a reality. We're going to let you go."

I said, "Fine." I mean, if you're going to get fired, you might as well be in L.A. I went to Santa Anita Race Track the next day and hung out for a while.

I never took it personally. In fact, I felt it was time to get out. As a coach in any sport, really, if you don't win in the first three or four years, things become more difficult. The players have a tough time listening to you, and some cease to buy into your system—and even try to figure it out on their own. They begin to doubt you. One guy in particular was questioning everything I did. He thought he was helping, but he wasn't. But that's the way it goes for coaches when their team is near the bottom in the standings for a prolonged period of time.

It was a strange situation all around. The Bruins wanted to keep Jean Ratelle, but fire Doakie and I. I told Harry that was wrong; to keep on an assistant coach and fire the others did not make sense. He agreed. However, when Doakie was apprised of the situation, he decided it wouldn't be right to stay on without me. So he accepted his walking papers, making it evident where his loyalty rests.

Jean stayed on while Harry took over as head coach for the remainder of the season.

That summer the New York Rangers coaching job was available. The late Herb Brooks, more known for leading the 1980 United States Olympic hockey team to the gold medal as their head coach, was fired midway through the 1984–85 season. He was replaced by the team's vice president and general manager, Craig Patrick. I went to New York to meet with Patrick about the job. The interview was at 3PM on a Friday. It must have been 100 degrees outside that day in the city. I took a shuttle in, met Patrick, and wrapped the meeting by 4PM. It was a nightmare trying to get to the airport at that time of day, but I did. I hopped on a shuttle and headed back to Boston, all the while thinking to myself, I hope they never call me.

Quite frankly, it was only money that could have lured me back to the bench, but even that wasn't enough for me. I was done.

That's the only interview I ever had for a head coaching job, which followed my stint with the Bruins as their boss.

As a coach I always had a terrific relationship with the front office of the Bruins, and especially with Harry Sinden. Contrary to popular belief, when Harry hired a coach, he let them coach. For some odd reason, the perception was always that he hired a guy as more of an extension himself, so he could run the show from the box. That wasn't the case with me, or any other guy as I recollect. Sure, he was a good guy to go to for advice, certainly. But never, not once, did he force me to play or sit anyone. He was a good man to work for.

In the end I can say this, my coaching career, like my playing career, was filled with ups and downs. Of course, I can argue there were more downs, considering we weren't able to win a Cup in the four plus years I was there. Nevertheless, it was a terrific experience, filled with excitement, sorrow, high drama, and tension; everything you would expect from being the head coach of the Boston Bruins.

My fondest memory came in the spring of 1983. After disposing of the Quebec Nordiques in the first round of the playoffs, we faced off against the Buffalo Sabres in a best of 7 series. We took a 3–2 lead in the series after a 9–0 thrashing given to Buffalo. But we fell in game 6, with a score of 5–3, which forced a game 7 back at our place. This set the stage for one heck of a game. That night the Garden would once again become the scene of one of the more memorable goals in NHL history.

It was overtime in that game 7. On a face-off in our offensive zone, Barry Pederson won the draw. Buffalo's goaltender, Bob Sauve, made a save when Brad Park let a slap shot go from the point. Everyone did a great job taking guys out of the play. Then, out of the scrum in front of the net, the puck trickled back to Park in the slot when he teed off another blast; the puck buzzed passed a pile of Sabres in front of the net and went in. Just before the face off I made a pretty nifty coaching move by shifting some guys around and it paid off as we got the goal and won the series.

The players did the work, though. They always did, and had a good time doing it.

One of my proudest moments as a couch involved Terry O'Reilly. Terry's nickname was, "The Tasmanian Devil." He was a tough guy who was full of piss and vinegar. On the wing, his point was always open, so I decided to make him a penalty killer. Truth be told, he became one of the very best I had ever seen, much to the delight of my wife, who was, and still is, a big Terry O'Reilly fan.

RETIREMENT

I knew if I had gone back to coaching, or at least explored other opportunities around the league, my efforts in finding a job would have been desultory at best. My heart wasn't in it. I still loved the game whole-heartedly. I always did and I always will. But I knew at this juncture, given all that coaching entailed—its responsibilities from dialing up the x's and o's, to the traveling, to God knows what else—I was ready for a break. I spent it the only way I knew how.

The Indian Ridge Country Club was a place that harbored the young golf enthusiasts, the fringe players, and the retirees looking for nothing more than some unremitting relaxation by building a rapport with the beautiful landscape and of course, its members. It was a place for good folks to let their hair down and worry about nothing but their score cards.

I had belonged to the club for a few years now. I was one of them. I made lots of friends on the course, resulting in some fun times away from the fairways.

Though my "vacation" had seemingly begun, to my eye it took on a similar look to most of my off seasons. I was socializing, hitting the links…enjoying life.

But the first year came and went with me assuming my role as a spectator, enjoying the occasional call-in to the radio stations, or brief television appearance for some interviews. I saw the Bruins endure another post-season defeat at the hands of the Canadiens; a 0–3 sweep in round 1.

Montreal ended up winning another one.

Had I been at the helm for that opening round series I would have taken a closer look, I guess.

But before the NHL handed the Cup over one more time, I was already happily ensconced on the fairways of Indian Ridge (IR) and other courses as I mapped out my leisure itinerary for the summer of 1986.

However, it was at IR where I'd once again be tempted by fate to make a return to hockey in a capacity I felt was well suited for me.

Indian Ridge had a member named Ron Ryan, who ran SportsChannel New England, the cable network that aired the Hartford Whalers games during this era.

Ron approached me one day and asked if I would be interested in the color commentator position calling the Whalers games. With little hesitation I acquiesced. I was game. I thought it was a great gig, an exciting one in which I'd be given a bird's-eye view of the world's best hockey players, and all I had to do was talk about it. Tell me where to sign.

So I took a drive down to Connecticut and interviewed with none other than Ron Ryan. I got the job. And for the second time in nearly two decades I'd be working under the umbrella of an organization not named the Boston Bruins. The beauty of it was, I didn't have to relocate outside of New England. In fact, I stayed in Massachusetts and commuted 1 hour, 40 minutes to work. If I was exhausted or the team had a game the next day, I'd sometimes grab a hotel room and stay overnight. But it worked out beautifully.

I had a sweet deal. I was paid per game, and each year that amount would go up by $100 per game. In the playoffs I'd get double.

Go Whalers!

Now I had to get to know the franchise.

The Whalers were an expansion club who came over from the WHA, but their inaugural campaign in the NHL began in '79. By that time the team stocked up on veteran talent, guys like Gordy Howe, Bobby Hull, and the WHA's all-time leading scorer, Andre Lacroix.

Now the Whalers could shed the image of being an organization filled with inexperienced, leftover deck hands to a team to be reckoned with.

The organization was run by General Manager, Emile Francis, a terrific guy. He always treated me well, as did the team's head coach, Jack Evans, another wonderful person.

My partner up in the booth was Rick Peckham. Rick was, and still is, a dear friend of mine, and still a great commentator; today he's the voice of the Tampa Bay Lightning. His career began on the airwaves with the Rochester Americans. In '84 he took over as the play-by-play man for the Whalers. To my eye, Rick is the ultimate professional as a broadcaster, the best in the business.

We had a lot of fun, Rick and I. He was the staunch enthusiast, and I was something else. I had a tendency to bring an unconventional style to the booth, often resulting in some levity on the air.

We called a nationally televised game between the Montreal Canadiens and the Quebec Nordiques, which was a big thing. It was one of the best rivalries in the business. As expected, the contest promised a major viewing of the audience, so we needed to be on point from the opening remarks until the close of the telecast. But at one point during the game, as I recall, the producer was counting down from 10 (we would be live in 10 seconds), when I began singing, "We're in the money. We're in the money." I was giddy for no obvious reason.

"No! No!" the producer shouted in my ear. "We're live!"

It was my first blooper and it happened on national television in front of a mass of devoted hockey fans from coast to coast. Rick didn't like it too much, as he was the tidy one with his words, a consummate professional.

I used to drive Rick nuts with some of the 'off the wall' things I used to say that may, or may not have, made much sense during games. Even by accident a linguistic folly would be blurted out, raising questions as to what I meant to say.

One time a Whalers player was parked in front of the net in his offensive zone, when the puck squirted out to him stealthily, unaware of anyone else involved in the play. The guy scored rather easily. When I gave my 2 cents on the play, I wanted to refer to the scorer as, "Johnny on the spot," but instead uttered, "He was Johnny on the pot!"

All I got were stares from Ricky, one after another.

During a game against Buffalo, in the closing minutes of the 3rd period, there was a face-off in the Sabre's zone. So instead of informing the public the referee was dropping the puck on the ice, I proudly said, "The face-off will be in Buffalo's dressing room."

A blunder, yes. But I was cognizant of the fact that, given the way the Sabres were positioned on the ice, they would be primed for a speedy and efficient exit to the locker room seconds later!

Another time one guy cut his nose on the ice while another lost his contacts. So I said, "They're looking for part of his nose."

It took some time, but eventually Ricky became accustomed to my humor, and even began to get it. However, I can understand how some of the other commentators calling other games for other teams would snicker every time I said something they considered offbeat in their eyes. But I didn't care, I did my job and entertained many along the way.

If there was a guy who understood me it was Joel Quenneville. He was a Whalers defenseman and a pretty good hockey player. Joe loved playing the game of hockey, but still, you'd never know it then, that he'd become one of the best coaches in the game. His career behind the bench hit a high note when his Chicago Blackhawks won the Stanley Cup in 2010.

We've remained good friends, even now, as I enjoy my retirement while Joe continues to lead the Blackhawks.

As I began to morph into a respected color-man in hockey, one thing remained unchanged, and that was the people's perception of me. My name was synonymous with the Boston Bruins, and rightly so. I spent many years in Boston making a name for myself as a pretty good goaltender and Stanley Cup champion. However, now I had a commitment to the Whalers. After all, I was let go by the Bruins, but more importantly, this was my opportunity to get into broadcasting. So, for the time being, my allegiance would toggle.

I became a big fan of the Whalers. I met a lot of great guys like Kevin Dineen, Ronnie Francis, and, of course, Joel Quenneville, and many others.

It just so happened, too, that the Bruins and Whalers had a nice little rivalry brewing in the mid-80s and I was right there to call it. What made it even more fortuitous was that Derek Sanderson was on the other side calling the games for NESN. If you tuned in to both telecasts you would have thought you were watching two different games. I'd call it one way, he'd call it another. Derek, naturally, hoped the puck bounced the Bruins' way, and I was his antithesis. That was a lot of fun.

In fact, my experience with the Whalers in its entirety was very enjoyable.

What I liked most about calling the Whalers games, however, was that I really enjoyed working with Rick Peckham. It was good to be with him everyday. We developed a great rapport and fed off each other on the air.

I didn't travel much with the team, and I had no issue acquiescing to that perk. Technically, I worked for the SportsChannel anyway, not the Whalers, so I was able to stay put most of the time, as I previously mentioned.

During my tenure with SportsChannel and the Whalers, not much had changed. In 1988 Emile Francis was replaced by my old teammate, Eddie Johnston. In 1992, Eddie was succeeded by Brian Burke. Still, my job seemed to remain unruffled. It wasn't until new ownership took over in 1994 that I felt the ground begin to tremor.

The team was purchased by Peter Karmanos, who was committed to winning, as evidenced by some of the personnel changes he made early on: He acquired Jimmy Carson and Steven Rice via free agency, and traded for Bruins' defenseman, Glenn Wesley. Yet by doing all this, it was the belief by many that he'd pack the team up and move to another city. Despite Karmanos' insistences on keeping the Whalers in Hartford, he did not. True to a lot of public suspicion, in 1997 Karmanos moved the Whalers to North Carolina, renaming the team the Carolina Hurricanes.

Rick and I were let go in 1995 because SportsChannel alleged we made too much money. We were replaced by guys making half as much. However, I contend that Karmanos just wanted to bring in his own people.

If there was a silver lining, it was the fact that I didn't have to impel my family to begin packing for the next destination. In fact, once I got word I was no longer calling the "shots" for Hartford, I began making my tee times. No sooner did I drive a ball down a fairway, Harry Sinden reached out to me and asked if I was interested in being a scout for the Bruins.

"Sure!" I said.

I wouldn't work as an amateur scout, so I wouldn't be signing anyone. My focus was more geared toward instant gratification for the organization. I scouted free agents, players who may have been available for trade, and those put on waivers.

Like the goalie's union, the scouting fraternity was pretty close-knit. As a result, I met a lot of great people, including Peter Mahovlich, who was a terrific hockey player for a number of teams, as well as the Montreal Canadiens back in the 70s. We traveled a lot together, and when we weren't working we made it a point to loosen our ties and socialize.

Peter and I have remained good friends ever since.

Brad Park began scouting for the New York Rangers, which worked out great. Brad, myself, and Peter would work together, and then Ricky Ley came along from time to time as a member of the Canucks' scouting staff.

During the spring and fall, we didn't have to show up to the games until about 7PM, so we used to play eighteen holes in the morning and afternoons. We played some great matches. We'd go to dinner, then work, and then it was off to the next city.

It was a good gig.

It was a job, though, that required a lot of writing of reports, which I wasn't really into. Yet I was always a phone call away, so I relied more on direct communication when I evaluated the talent.

But I was really into the position. I was extremely competitive by nature, so I lived and died with every move I made.

In the midst of my scouting responsibilities, NESN had hired Phil Esposito to the games, but there was a conflict with Phil, as he was still under contract with Fox Sports. So, I stepped in until the situation was resolved. I called twenty or so games with a few different partners, including Dave Shea.

Dave was a terrific guy and great to work with. He called a lot of national and NCAA hockey for ESPN and Hockey East.

In 2000 the club pulled off its most barefaced move by trading away Ray Bourque to the Colorado Avalanche.

When Harry Sinden stepped down as the general manager of the club, Mike O'Connell stepped in.

It was good working for Mike. He played a role in the Joe Thornton trade which sent the veteran forward to San Jose for forwards Marco Sturm and Wayne Primeau, and defenseman Brad Stuart.

Unlike the Thornton trade wherein the Bruins only dealt with one team, the Bourque deal was something else.

I wasn't heavily involved in the transaction, as none of the guys I scouted were part of the package. But it was the first time I had seen Sinden work the phones. He was isolated in a room, uttering his demands specific to each call he picked up, and there were many. It was something.

Naturally, that trade garnered much attention around hockey.

Perhaps, the most prolific transaction I was a part of was in 1997 when the Bruins traded Adam Oates, along with Bill Ranford and Rick Tocchet to the Washington Capitals for Jim Carey, Anson Carter, and Jason Allison, as well as a mid-round draft pick.

It was a blockbuster trade that I believe paid dividends for Boston.

In 2006 new management came in. Harry was more of an advisor at this point. The new brass wanted their own, which was understandable. And with that, a lot of us were let go. But after eleven years it was time to step down.

With no immediate plans of going back to work, I began making plans to move to Florida. My wife and I found a nice place on the east coast of the Sunshine State. We moved in and have never looked back, except to witness the Bruins win the Stanley Cup in 2011.

I was cheering like heck for them. I thought it was great. I had never seen a team who wouldn't say no like the 2011 Boston Bruins. When they were down 0–2 to Vancouver, I thought they were a cinch to win. The B's were "getting it." They knew they were tougher than the Canucks, and put it right to them. Even when they were down 2–3 you just knew they would force a game 7. They approached the final game like real champs; they deserved to win.

It was a terrific victory for them. The Bruins weren't favorites going in, but if you were to take a step back and ask yourself, which team had a certainty in goal and which team did not, the answers would have been obvious.

The Bruins got tremendous goaltending by Tim Thomas. He read everything perfectly in that series against Vancouver. Timmy was as dominant as any goaltender I have ever witnessed in the Stanley Cup finals. He even played great in the games they lost. I remember watching Patrick Roy and Martin Brodeur at the top of their games in the post season. Thomas' play in the 2011 playoffs was very much comparable to them, if not, his performance was better, especially in the finals.

What made it sweeter for Tim Thomas is to consider his trek to the NHL. Mike O'Connell brought him in due to an injury sustained by then goaltender John Grahame.

Media and fans alike expressed disdain over the signing, affirming Thomas made too much money.

How about now?

Now, he's the best goalie in the game. He has talent, great character, and a lot of heart.

Thomas epitomized what a journeyman really is. From college to the AHL to Finland to the Bruins there were always doubts as to whether he would ever solidify himself as an NHL goaltender. Ultimately, he did, in a big way, becoming a Stanley Cup champion.

People ask me now if there are any comparisons to the Cup-winning

Bruins of the 70s and the 2011 Boston team, but I don't do that. I think it's unfair to both teams. They are their own team and that's the way it should be. They don't have Bobby Orr or Phil Esposito, but they have great players in their own right.

What I could contrast is the parade, how much fun these guys have playing the game, and even how they engage the fans.

Today's Bruins team has great leadership, as did the Cup-winning teams I was on.

As far as drawing any comparisons between Tim Thomas and me, I'm not going there.

Again, it wouldn't be fair. I will say this: Thomas is a great goaltender. He gets out there, all over the ice and he handles the puck like some of the forwards do. It's a rare skill that when it goes awry can get a goalie in big trouble.

Patrick Roy was a terrible puck handler. He was like a blacksmith out there. When I saw him in junior hockey he couldn't handle the puck. He improved slightly over time, but never became reliable.

Overall, it's very difficult comparing one goaltender to the next. Each net minder has his style, build, and mind-set. But all with one thing in common: to stop the puck.

Patrick Roy was big, imposing, and able to always cut the angle; he also had the ability to shut a team down. Martin Brodeur in my opinion is the best goaltender in the modern era. Martin stands up, plays the angle, is good with the puck, and is always in good position. Then, along came Dominick Hassek, who, like Timmy, was very mobile and always knew where the puck was.

The Bruins had a goalie named Jim Carey. He had great skills and was very athletic, but half the time he had no idea where the puck was. He became a reaction goalie, a method that usually leads to a shortened career.

Equipment undoubtedly played a role in the evolution of the goaltender. Guys today are covered in armor from head to toe. I remember when Byron Dafoe, after he had a very good year, said to me, "I have to get bigger."

I said, "But you also need to move."

Jean-Sebastian Giguere, the goalie for the Anaheim Ducks when they won the Cup in 2007, could read plays very well, and he was big. So he'd locate the puck, get in position, and let it hit him. The puck would find him, and he'd be recorded with a save.

Don't get me wrong, that was good goaltending, but another example of a guy who adapted to his strengths and molded a style that worked for him. Unflappable, he seemed, but it worked.

These days every team has a goalie coach. They watch hours of video, analyzing and coming up with thoughts and conclusions on how to improve their pupil's performance. Goalies can't help but play better now.

Some goalies, I believe, are over coached. Some don't have to be coached at all.

Mitch Korn coached Dominick Hassek for a period of time. Mitch is one of the best goalie coaches in hockey. He's a great guy, and quite a character.

If you watch Hassek, you'll find that this guy knows where the puck is at all times, as well as any goalie in history. I spoke to Mitch about Hassek and his approach to teaching him, and he said, "I didn't have to coach him any. I just motivated him."

Mitch didn't have to teach him basic goaltending. For example, stand on your feet and cut the angle down. He made sure Dominick knew where the puck was, and he got in position to stop it.

The Bruins' coach, Bob Essensa, is a great goalie coach.

I never had a goalie coach.

I let in a bad goal in Pittsburgh when Harry Sinden was coaching. After the goal, Sinden sent out Teddy Green, just after he told him, "Tell Gerry to stay on his feet!" I got so mad at that, I broke my stick on a guy's ankle as he skated across the crease. I went to the bench, and saw Harry run to the other end as I rifled my stick in his direction.

That was the extent of me having a goalie coach.

And I won't have one any time soon because I'm retired. If an opportunity arose where I'd be asked to come back to hockey in some capacity, quite frankly, my answer would be "no."

I still keep in touch with the many friends I've made over the years. In fact, a good portion of them made their dwelling down here in Florida.

I still golf; I golf a lot. I play five times a week at a beautiful course in Florida. I'm having the time of my life.

I very much enjoy watching my grandson play hockey, especially now, since he's a little older and he's understanding the game more. He really loves to play. He's currently playing for the Florida Junior Panthers.

I travel north to Boston and Canada several times a year to see friends and family. However, on a somber note, as I write this book in its latter stages, my mother passed away at the age of 96.

As far as business, I have nothing. However, I gave my partner and friend, Steve Cardillo, of Cardillo Weight Belts and American Nutrition Center in Everett, MA, the rights to www.gerrycheevers.com. He manufactures and sells a replica of my mask to the public. Things are going wonderfully for him.

I'm still, and always will be, a strong supporter of Cystic Fibrosis. As a matter of fact, my whole family is involved in the fight, as my son, Robby, and his wife, Kim, have two daughters, Laura and Cate, who have CF. They're terrific kids, and just a joy to be around.

There have been breakthroughs of late, which is why we believe that raising money works.

We do an annual walk in Andover, Massachusetts, along with three to four other events—all in the hope to raise money to give each person with the disease a better life. My son Robby and daughter Sherril both run in the Boston Marathon to raise money.

Hats off to Gord Kluzak, who runs a pool tournament and golf tournament each year, raising an awful lot of money in the fight against CF. Joe O'Donnell is an entrepreneur from the Boston area who leads the fight against CF and runs the Joey Fund. Together these guys raised more than $100 million.

Because of the efforts of Gord, Joe, and many others, researchers have made incredible strides toward finding a cure.

Finally, hats off to all who nurtured me, coached me, guided me, cheered for me, and supported me along my journey in hockey from the ponds of St. Catharines to the Garden ice. Your loyalty, love, and respect have always been, and will forever be, deeply and sincerely appreciated.

Thank you, all.

THE MASK

For the better part of my career I never wore a mask. It wasn't the exception, it was the norm. The guy who first donned a face shield in pro hockey was Jacques Plante. It was homemade, and more closely resembled that of a tool commonly used to prevent mentally ill patients from harming someone, including themselves, with their "chompers." Jacques, however, had other ideas. He'd taken a puck to the face, consequently shattering his nose. When he returned after having been stitched up in the locker room, Jacques sported a mask for the first time.

Slowly but surely, a brigade followed with some of the most oddly and incongruous styles of head gear, ultimately putting the goaltending position on a new course.

I wore a practice mask in juniors. It was flimsy, made of thin, transparent plastic that fogged up something terrible. Had I held my breath for more than 60 minutes at a time, I guess that problem could have been averted. But that was unlikely. So I used a mask in practice, in juniors, but never in the games.

Gradually, though, I came to realize, if I wanted to continue to play hockey beyond juniors, I was going to need to protect the noggin. I had taken a few lumps before, but all it takes is one in the right spot to change the way a man thinks about his future. The future was now.

I began to experiment, and the first was a Lefty Wilson Mask. It was made from fiberglass, had no anchor near the chin, so every time I got hit the mask shifted, thus obstructing my line of sight. That wasn't going to work, because as everyone knows, the ability to see is a pretty important faculty to possess for a goaltender.

But I kept at it year after year, trying to find the right one. I experimented on the side with different shapes; some bigger, some even fashioned as helmets. Finally, when I went to Boston I met a man named Ernie Higgins. Ernie came up with the idea of putting an anchor on the chin so the mask wouldn't shift. Higgins took his idea to the workshop when he built me one, anchor installed. Now, I was ready for action. That was the only type of mask I ever used. I had a few others made each year, carbon copies that I used during practice, but for the games there was only one.

The protection the mask afforded me gave me more time on the ice and less time in the locker room getting stitched up, which was nice. However, I hated the color of that thing. It was white. I hated white. I seldom even wore white socks. And if I happened to look down when I did, I felt a fright as if I was exposed to something with ill consequences. Call it what you want: A phobia, or outright disdain for this wholesome shade. The sight of this glimmering, shiny, white mold engaged to my facial pores drove me nuts. The color itself is a sign of purity and that wasn't me. I was quite the opposite. In fact, I was driven by an unconventional thought process and a wayward nature my whole life; the white had to go.

In my leisure time in the Garden I pranced around with my black sweat pants, black and gold shirt, and black socks—only to put on a white mask?

One morning I tried to get out of practice, which, again, was the norm for me, not the exception. I was in net when a puck flipped up and grazed the mask. The puck's force was so softly propelled, that, had I not been wearing the mask I seriously doubt I'd have so much as a scratch on my face. It was weak, but I faked like it wasn't. I winced in pain, came off the ice, and headed into the dressing room. I sat down and sparked up a cigarette when Harry Sinden came in and said, "Get your ass out there, you're not hurt!"

So, before I collected myself and got back on the ice, Frosty the trainer said, "Here, hold it."

Frosty broke out a sharpie and drew in 4 or 5 stitches where I had undoubtedly been hit, right above my eye, I believe it was. Everyone got a kick out of it, so I told Frosty, "Fros, every time I get hit with a puck, or the stick comes up, take care of it." He did, and all the marks were legit. One shot I'd never forget.

Willy Huber was a giant on the ice. At 6'5 his presence was noted. Conversely, I don't believe he was ever credited with having one of the hardest slap shots in hockey. One day I felt like maybe he was well deserving of such an honor. The puck trickled right to him. He teed it up and rifled one right off my nose. That one I felt. And believe me, just because I had a mask on, doesn't mean I put my face in front of the puck every chance I got. That one hurt, and if I'd had the chance to get out of the way of it, I would have. I would have played it differently.

The following day in practice, after the ceremonial stitch was placed across the white of my nose, Ernie Higgins, the mask's architect, marveled at how well it withstood the blast.

Ernie was a serious guy. I was not. So I told him, the fiberglass from the mask was getting in the defenseman's eyes every time the puck hit it. I had him going for awhile, thinking a change needed to be made. The mask took a beating, but it held up nicely.

To my eye, the mask was nothing more than a little artwork being applied to this dreadful obstruction resting between the puck and my face. Thank goodness we did something about it, though, because who knows what would have happened had we not become pioneers in the art of decorating the goalie mask. Maybe "pioneer" is my idea of a hyperbole. However, today it's pretty evident how much work now goes into transforming the goaltender's headgear into a work of art. Goalies were going to decorate their masks eventually anyway, I just sped up the process.

So, first came the mask, then, came the antics.

Don Cherry loved his dog, Blue, his white Bull Terrier. The dog was infamous. He was a gift from the Bruins' players, but the way Grapes coddled him you'd think the gift came down from Olympus.

Blue later became a star when he landed a reoccurring role, playing himself, on Grape's shows, Don Cherry's Rock'em, Sock'em Hockey and The Grapevine.

The four-legged prince of Boston was to be taken care of by one of the trainers while the team was on the ice practicing. It was a chore not so highly coveted by the staff, but viewed as towering on their list of responsibilities.

It should be noted that I never wore my game mask during practice. Instead, I used a slightly larger one for more protection.

We were scrimmaging one day, when in the middle of the practice we all looked up to see Blue, slipping and sliding everywhere, donning my mask, helplessly trying to keep his balance. I actually felt bad for the pooch. Grapes went nuts chewing out Frosty, but as an onlooker, you couldn't help but find the incident comical. Even Grapes did, when his fury eventually subsided.

The mask and its mystique came with me when I jumped leagues over to the WHA. Believe it or not, comparisons are drawn to other goaltenders' designs now.

I remember a goalie named Gilles Gratton, a.k.a., "Gratoony the Loony." What a character. He was way out there, and he even told a few of his teammates he was reincarnated and was once in the Spanish Inquisition.

He was a brilliant pianist, though. He once heard the Russian national anthem, and subsequently played the same tune on the keys like he'd been doing it for years.

So, not only was he recognized for his irregular character, skills as a goaltender, and musical prowess, but Gilles Gratton also had one of the scariest masks in hockey. It was a picture of a lion—a pretty angry one.

Aside from Gratton, early on, not too many guys were into decorating the masks. Most, in fact, were content on putting their team logo on them.

When I got back from the WHA the Bruins had a game against the Kansas City Scouts. They had a guy named Denis Dupere. I never heard of him, but I found out he was quite a comic.

During the game I got hit in the head with the puck; not the hardest shot, but hard enough. I went down, and was in a sort of daze when Denis Dupere (who, again, I had never heard of before in my life) skated up to me and asked, "Want me to run and get a Sharpie?"

"Nah, I'm alright," I told him.

It was a privilege to draw the scar, and one man I would have given the honor to rode a horse.

Jimmy Davern was a jockey and racing official in New England back in the day. He was also a dear friend of mine.

Jimmy was into all kinds of primitive artwork, and had a tremendous eye for all things born from creative forethought. So, naturally, Davern had a great interest, and great appreciation for my mask, and asked if he could have it as part of his extensive collection.

I gave him a mask, all drawn up, but never used in a game. Jimmy proudly displayed the mask in his home.

Unfortunately, Jimmy Davern passed away too quickly. But in his last act of thoughtfulness, in his will, he left me my mask.

He was a good friend and a terrific person.

No other notables were privy to taking ownership like Jimmy was. But I recall a Dennis Leary celebrity hockey game when Michael J. Fox (before his Parkinson's disease unfortunately took control of his life) asked if he could have a picture of the mask for his son. Of course, I obliged.

Who delivered the blow, causing the sharpie to be summoned one last time?

I have no idea.

My last game, though, was against the Islanders in the post season. I hurt my knee, came out, and never returned. So I suppose it could have been someone skating for New York that day or in that series.

Brian Trottier?

Denis Potvin, perhaps?

I have no idea.

If anyone has an idea, don't be shy, shout it out!

Today, the original rests on my grandson's wall. However, many were left behind. A fact well noted when I caught wind of the Bruins' selling them off when the Boston Garden was being torn down. I was a little disturbed, but, what the heck, I never actually bought any of them anyway.

I had a bunch of masks over the years that never made it to a game, too. I had two made up at the start of every year for emergencies, or training camp and exhibition games. Those particular masks, however, had smaller holes for my eyes, so when I went out there to play in the game, I'd have a more 'wide open' view of what was going on.

I lost track of each mask over the years, aside from the one my grandson has. There was another one that I gave to my friend, Steve Cardillo, who then gave it to a construction worker to be dropped in the foundation for the new Garden. There's probably a lot of stuff nestled deep inside the earth beneath where the B's skate today.

Whatever the case, never in a million years would I have supposed the mask to be so talked about so many years later, and be forever adored by fans everywhere as one of hockey's most memorable images. I've recognized through the years it's been near or at the top of many polls to see who had the best, most unique, or most identifiable mask in NHL history. Because of its vintage look and uniqueness, it'll probably stay that way.

And you'll never see anyone wearing that type of mask, stitches or not, in a game today. They'd have to be nuts. It offered little protection. It had oversized eye slots and no protection for the back of my head, or anything beneath my chin.

Goalies now have become competitive with their décor, and continue to strive toward having the game's most unique, picturesque artwork right in front of their faces. However, any discussion of masks always comes back to the mask with the stitches. It doesn't make much sense to me, to be quite honest, but that's the way it's been. In fact, I still get letters from kids from places like Sweden, Czechoslovakia, and other countries across the world, asking how they can get a mask with the stitches on it.

Even now, on occasion, I'll be introduced to someone as a former Boston Bruin, the guy with the mask.

"Oh, yeah!" I hear a lot, which is okay. It'd be nice if they remembered me for playing twenty-one years as a pro, and winning a couple of Stanley Cups, though, but what the heck.

A FEW CHARACTERS

Niagara Falls, Ontario, Canada, late August of 2011 was the place and time; Gerry and I loomed upon the latter stages of *Unmasked*. The interviewing, editing and research had neared its end. And with an eye on the book's conclusion, we both sat on his deck, firmly situated on our respective lawn chairs, each enjoying a few beers after a round of golf. We sat for a while sharing our thoughts, deliberating, even debating what the final act of this project should reflect.

"Tell me more about Bobby Orr." I said.

He did.

I leaned back in my chair, closed my eyes and pondered a bit.

"Sanderson", I muttered.

Gerry went on about Derek. Then, I asked about Harry Sinden, Grapes, Gerry Pinder and a few others. I asked, he told. That's how it happened that day.

The setting had its serenity; its stillness, but the rap session was priceless. Though my score card may suggest otherwise, it really was a perfect ending to a perfect day.

And so I anointed our last conversation regarding *Unmasked*, the autobiography of Gerry Cheevers, as its sincere conclusion.

So, here are Gerry's final thoughts…

Don "Grapes" Cherry

I first bumped into Grapes back in 1963 in Rochester with the Americans. We had nothing in common, not a thing, but we hit it off right away and became very good friends.

Grapes was a good defenseman. With Don Cherry on the ice, I never had a problem locating a second shot. I saw everything so well.

And Grapes was old-time hockey, and one of the toughest players I had ever seen.

In that game in Providence when Grapes and Spider Mazur collided, got up, dropped their sticks and gloves, and went at it. The two brawlers went back in the dressing room, got sewn up, and went back out there.

I thought to myself, "Wow! These guys are tough."

I always hooted anytime Grapes started bashing the Europeans, calling them chicken and anything else to refer to their lack of toughness. I felt bad for some of the guys from over there, because not all of them were as wimpy as Grapes said they were. But at the same time, none of them could play with Cherry. He was all-out and the toughest guy on the ice at all times.

As much as I enjoyed playing with Grapes—he was a very good teammate—playing for him was even more enjoyable. I could hardly get to the rink fast enough when Don coached me up in Boston. Every day I had the feeling that something offbeat was going to happen. Every day was an adventure. It was a great atmosphere, even in practice; and that says a lot.

But one time in the playoffs against the Canadiens, Bobby Miller showed up to the arena with a blistering sunburn. Bobby wasn't complaining, but Grapes took one look at it and expressed his displeasure.

"You can't have a sunburn in the playoffs!" Grapes said. "You have to look white and pale like the rest of us! Get rid of it!"

Grapes, in some abnormal way, was serious. He would have loved it if Bobby somehow made the tan disappear. But that wasn't going to happen.

My Dad

He was a car salesman, and a very good one. He sold most of his cars out of the Canadian Legion, which was more closely compared to an Elk's club.

Every Christmas or New Year's, the Legion would throw a holiday party, and whenever there was leftover excitement, dad would bring the crew back to our house. He used to play the piano, but he only knew one song, "Let Me Call You Sweetheart." And no matter what song was sung, "Silent Night" or "Little Drummer Boy," dad would play "Let Me Call You Sweetheart" on the piano.

I played lacrosse for him a couple of times, and he was the best coach I ever had in the sport.

Dad was a "gentleman-scoundrel."

One time we were playing against the Buffalo Sabres, and my dad decided to bring a bunch of kids to the game to meet some of the players. Well, not only did he bring the group to our dressing room, he took them over to the Sabres' dressing room as well.

That was my dad. Nothing bothered him.

Wayne Cashman

I played a couple of games with Bert Olmstead up in Toronto. To me, Olmstead and Wayne Cashman were the two best corner guys you'll ever see in hockey.

"Cash" was a great teammate, and a very smart person. He always had a great answer to any question you threw him, which added a bit to his sense of humor.

Cash did impressions, but they all sounded like John Wayne. Whether it was James Cagney or anyone else, it ended up sounding like John Wayne.

He was a good teammate and a character, and a very important part of the team.

Bobby Orr

Bobby Orr, along with Cash, was a great teammate. But when you win Stanley Cups, there are a lot of great teammates involved.

During a game in New York when we were ahead 3–0, Cash fed Bobby in front of the net and scored. Orr then said to Cash, "Nice tip-in."

"Of course," Cash said. "It's your goal."

"Just take the goal," Bobby insisted.

That's the kind of guy Orr was.

On the ice, Orr's skills were unmistakable. In warm-ups he used to ask me where I wanted the puck. I told him once, "Go stick side." Bobby would shoot it and I'd save it.

"That wasn't even close," I said to him. So, Bobby would call for the puck.

"Where do you want it?"

I said, "Go stick side, post."

The next thing you hear is clank! Off the post, stick side. He could do anything.

Off the ice, he was the ultimate team player, who really cared about winning.

Frosty

Frosty was our trainer along with Dan Canney.

When I became coach of the Bruins, we had an exhibition game in Rhode Island. I had my son Craig take the bus along with the rookies. When we got home I saw Frosty and Danny arguing to the point where I thought they'd end up on the floor throwing fists. That night around 1AM I went home with my son, but I remember saying, "I really need to straighten this thing out." So, I got back in there in the morning, and before I could say anything, I saw them helping each other and being very cordial toward one another. They looked like long lost brothers. Apparently the beef between the two of them was the norm. They argued every night, and in the morning they'd act as if it never happened.

Frosty had a helper, a little guy who was nicknamed "Tattoo" for his diminutive stature. Frosty treated him much like Benny Hill treated the little guy on The Benny Hill Show.

One time Frosty locked his keys in his apartment, which was located above a bar called The Fours in Boston. Well, Frosty came to the conclusion that the only way to get in was to go through the window. So, Patty Considine was waiting on the third floor for Frosty to yell up to him, while Tattoo was tied to a rope. The plan was to run down a hallway and fling Tattoo up to the window. As strong as Patty was, Tattoo fell about eight feet short and hit the building flush.

One time in a game in L.A., as the crowd was attempting to listen to the national anthem, the sound was knocked out of the mic. Someone, I'm not saying who, sabotaged the feed.

Frosty, in my opinion, was the most important non-hockey player member on the team.

Phil Esposito

Phil was one of the greatest goal scorers in history. And one thing he will never admit is that "Espo" was a great penalty killer. But still he had the greatest desire to score goals of anyone I've ever met.

There were times we didn't see eye-to-eye, for example, when we had big leads. One time we were beating St. Louis 6–0, and Espo, Cash, and "Hodgie" (Kenny Hodge) are trying to get a seventh goal. But they'd leave the ice open and I'd see a three-on-one; I made some saves, but I remember letting a goal in with about 15 seconds left. I was pissed. I took some guy's helmet off and got a 5-minute penalty. Espo's line was afraid to go in the dressing room when I was in there. They were hiding. They knew I did not like it. But it was water under the bridge.

Derek Sanderson

People always identified Derek as being a flamboyant, tough character, but Derek was a terrific hockey player. He scored 29 goals one year and all he did was kill penalties and play on the checking line. That's how good he was. And for a guy who wasn't as big as most on the ice, he was as tough as they come.

Derek was the most popular Bruin when I played with him. But he was a product of what people wanted him to be. He had some problems in life, but he worked hard and he's doing great.

He was always a character. And Derek rubbed elbows with the best. One time he asked me if I was interested in listening to Paul Anka rehearse. The singer was from Canada, so I said, "Sure, why not?"

We took a $70 cab ride to where we needed to go. Derek says, "Cheese, pick up the cab." Meanwhile, Paul Anka is waiting for us in his Rolls-

Royce. He took us in and we watched him sing with Shirley Bassey, the woman who sang "Goldfinger." It was a great experience. We got home and I picked up the cab again. Nice time, despite spending nearly $150 in cab fare.

Harry Sinden

I first met Harry in Oklahoma. We won a championship there.

Harry was an outstanding coach. In fact, along with Joe Crozier, Father Bauer, and Don Cherry, I would say they were the four most influential coaches I ever had. They were all different in their own way. Harry prided himself on being professional; he was always crossing his T's and dotting his I's. Psychologically, I would say Harry's approach to running a team ran parallel to Father Bauer's.

One year I played about thirty games in a row because Eddie Johnston got hurt. At the tail end of the streak while in Minnesota I went out for a couple of much-needed beers. At about 1AM, Harry said to me, "You stay out, we'll go in." He knew I needed some serenity.

Johnny McKenzie

Johnny McKenzie was a spark plug. He fit the persona of our Bruins team to the hill.

We're at the end of a long road trip, and Johnny and I went in for a massage in Montreal. We had this big, strapping Danish guy rubbing us down. He asks Johnny, "What do you do?"

Johnny replies, "I'm a hockey player."

Johnny is built like an upside-down pyramid. He has a tremendous body, so the Danish guy says, "Oh, I can see that. I can see that."

Then it was my turn. He asks me, "What do you do?"

"I'm a hockey player," I tell him.

"Come on, what do you really do?" he asks.

My body wasn't impressive, I guess.

Johnny Bucyk

Bucyk was the captain.

Johnny had a strong body, and had a knack for getting good position in front of the net to knock in rebounds or get passes.

But the "Chief", as he was called, was the guy who looked after everyone when they came to town. He could get you a deal on anything. That's all he cared about, getting deals. If you needed it, he'd get it, too.

Johnny liked to arrange all the parties. Again, he got the best deals he could for whatever was needed.

Freddy Stanfield

Freddy was a "suave-type" center, very smooth. He could pass the puck. He was a good playmaker, and he fit his line perfectly.

Off the ice he was a rather quiet guy. We played a lot of golf together, though, in St. Catharines, when he was my neighbor.

Kenny Hodge

Kenny Hodge was a very important part of the Cashman-Espo line. He was as strong as they came, and sometimes didn't know his own strength.

Kenny and Phil always got along really well, but their relationship was very important, so that was a good thing. It was key to them being so successful on the same line.

Donny Marcotte

Donny was very quiet, but an excellent team guy. And he was one of the hardest hitters you have ever seen. He was the first guy willing to take the body.

Donny, Eddie Westfall, and Derek made up a third line that was pretty damn good, and one of the best checking lines you will ever see in hockey. They all took pride in what they did out there.

Gary Doak

"Doakie" was my roommate for many years, and a very fun teammate. He was the brunt of many jokes, but he tried hard; in fact, no one worked harder than him. He was like a fart in a mitt out there.

Typically on a 3-1, the defenseman is the guy trying to force the pass for someone to take the shot. When Doakie was the defenseman, all you could hear was him yelling, "I got him! I got him! I got him!" Doakie tried to take on all three guys coming up the ice.

To this day we're still very close.

Eddie Johnston

Eddie was my first roommate when I went to Boston. We were both goalies, so we hit it off right away. He was actually very important in my development as a goaltender; he knew a lot about playing the position.

Eddie said to me, "The farther you come out of the net, the lower you get hit with the puck." One time in Chicago, Dennis Hull was coming straight at me on a three-on-one, but I couldn't blitz him because I would have left the net open. He took a shot that hit my shoulder and I went down like a ton of bricks. Eddie came out to the net to tell me, "I told ya, you have to blitz him!" Thank God there was only fifteen seconds left in the period.

But all Eddie cared about was winning. For me, he was the perfect guy to be teammates with, given his dedication and his position.

Terry O'Reilly

I didn't play much with Terry, but as it was, he and I had opposite interests outside of hockey, so we didn't mingle too much. Truth be told, I enjoyed coaching Terry more than anything. In fact, I remember my first game behind the bench. There was Terry all over the ice, living up to his nickname, "The Tasmanian Devil."

Terry developed into a top hockey player through his determination, hard work and effort.

He was also very conscientious, and stubborn, which he'll admit today.

Terry was certainly a tough guy to win an argument with. I told my wife, "That Terry O'Reilly…I'm going to have a long conversation with him." I got my wife all riled up. I said, "You know what the first thing I'm going to say to him is?"

"What?" she asked.

I said, "Terry, don't hang up on me."

And that was my approach. I figured the phone was safer.

When I coached him, I decided to make him a penalty killer.

He was a great team guy, and was involved with some of the best fights you'll ever see in hockey.

In retirement we still see each other. Terry just got married and we wish him well.

Ricky and Dallas Smith

Dallas and Ricky Smith were a couple of my favorite defensemen. I loved playing behind him. He had a knack for forcing a guy to take a shot from a weak angle. We won a lot together in Oklahoma City. We just knew how to play defense together.

Ricky Smith was much of the same. He always seemed to bounce the puck out of harms way when we needed it most.

They were a couple of underrated defensemen, but two of my favorite defensemen I ever played with.

Garnet "Ace" Bailey

Ace was a talent. He could skate and shoot well. In fact, I always had a tough time picking up his shot. And if we were in practice and Bobby decided not to have the puck most of the time, Ace would have been the one skating around with it. Ace was the guy spending an extra fifteen minutes before and after morning skates to improve his skills.

We used to have some pretty good arguments when the puck got away from him, but he was a fun guy to have on the team. He was a lot of laughs. We all miss him, of course.

Phil "Skippy" Krake

Skippy Krake was a quiet assassin-type of player. He was good, a tough player.

I remember when he and Dallas Smith got called up from Oklahoma City and Hap Emms says to everyone, "Well, team, this is it, the bottom of the barrel." But that was more of a reflection on the GM than it was on Skippy and Dallas.

We were fortunate to have those guys on the team as they each played a big role in winning two championships in a row with Oklahoma City.

To this day, Skippy still enjoys having a beer and a cigarette and just having a good time. He and his wife, Diane, and my wife and I have remained very good friends over the years.

Paul Shmyr and Gerry Pinder

No one flew under the radar like Paul Shmyr. He was as tough a defenseman as I ever played with, but for some reason, he never got the credit he deserved. He got the job done moving the puck up the ice, and he was the best player the Cleveland Crusaders had by a mile. Shmyr came over with Gerry Pinder from the Blackhawks.

When I was with the Bruins, we lost to Chicago one game 1–0 with Eddie Johnston in goal. "Pindie" scored the lone goal. But I swore it wasn't in. He swore it was in. There was no instant replay in the booth back then, so once the light went on, the score stood. I think the Blackhawks ended up finishing in first place by a point that year.

Pindie made his mark in Cleveland, too.

He was a slick left winger and a very good two-way player who learned his hockey in Hockey Canada. He was very methodical when he went down the ice. Pindie was also one of the many characters we had on the Cleveland Crusaders.

I remember the first game we played on the road with Cleveland in

Los Angeles against the Sharks, who were supposedly a team full of "tough guys." That particular game, every opposing player took a swing at him, but went back to the bench to get a new stick after they broke their own, trying to hack away at Pindie, but Gerry got the best of it. I never saw anything like it. All five guys broke their stick over Pindie.

We all became pretty close friends. We had some good times. I was very fortunate to have met these guys in Cleveland.

Sadly, Paul Shmyr passed away a few years back with throat cancer.

Normie Corcoran

Normie Corcoran was a terrific guy who lived in St. Catharines. I learned so much from him about how to be a professional hockey player. When I was sent to Rochester, he was already there. I followed Normie around like a little puppy dog. But he liked to go to the races, and so did I. In fact, we both worked at Fort Erie Race Track in the summers.

Normie was maybe one of the best lacrosse players in Canada. I played on a line with him and learned so much from him.

He was a top hockey player as well. Normie was in the Bruins organization and eventually played under Eddie Shore for the AHL's Springfield Indians. He was a very good minor league hockey player. Today he would be a terrific player in the NHL.

Normie was simply a guy I was very fortunate to know.

Red Armstrong

I met Red in Sudbury, Ontario, playing for the Wolves.

Red was noted as being a guy who loved to fight inside of five minutes left in a game, so he wouldn't have to come back out. I never saw him after a game until I got to a bar, because he had already showered, dressed, and gone by the time the rest of the team got back to the dressing room.

Red was the most popular player in the history of the Rochester Americans.

One of his coaches, I believe it was "Peanuts" O'Flaherty, traded him to Baltimore. When Red came back to play the Americans, after he scored a goal, he skated past O'Flaherty and flicked his hat off with his stick.

Most remember Red for scoring a goal in just seven seconds on his first shift in the NHL for the Leafs. During a Hockey Night in Canada game.

Murph Chamberlain

Murph was my coach in Sudbury. He liked me personally, but he didn't like the way I went about my life. I was out of shape, so he was always on me about my weight. But I wasn't the only one he got on.

I remember a playoff game against Ottawa. One of our players took a shot that went in the net, but came out back in play for a good minute to a minute and a half, so everyone continued on with the game. When the play stopped we couldn't find Murph. He was down at the other end of the ice in a fight with the goal judge. He pulled him under the cage and beat the hell out of him for not putting the red light on.

When Murph was a player for the Canadiens, he was in charge of a couple of younger players. One night when the train stopped, these couple of guys got off the train to grab some refreshments. When they came back outside, they hopped on the wrong train. They were supposed to go to New York, but headed in the opposite direction, as far away from the city as one can get!

"I noticed in Gerry's team picture that there was a third goaltender crouching clandestinely in the front row, last man on the right from my view. A lot of people do not know much about him. I know nothing about him. So, I asked Gerry to tell me a little bit about John Adams, the Bruins third goaltender."

~ Marc Zappulla

John Adams

Every team in hockey brought up a third goalie for the playoffs, so John came up from Oklahoma City in 1972.

He was a quiet guy from Thunder Bay, Ontario, Canada.

I talk to John occasionally, and I believe he's doing some recruiting work for Bobby Orr Enterprises Ltd, which represents players.

INDEX